MILITARY MEMOIR

OF

LIEUT. COL. JAMES SKINNER, C.B.

MILITARY MEMOIR

OF

LIEUT. COL. JAMES SKINNER, C.B.

J. BAILLIE FRASER, Esq.

IN TWO VOLUMES.

VOL.II.

Published by

Gyan Publishing House
5, Ansari Road
Daryaganj, New Delhi-110002
Phone: 011-47034999, 9811692060
E-mail: books@gyanbooks.com

Distribution Network
gyanbooks.com
India, USA, Canada, UK, Australia, France

ISBN : 978-81-212-9500-0 (Set)
978-81-212-9498-0 (PB)
First Published, 1851

2nd Impression 2023

Printed at: Gyan Press, Delhi.

**MILITARY MEMOIR OF LIEUT. COL. JAMES
SKINNER, C.B. (VOL-II)**
Author: J. BAILLIE FRASER

L.ᵗ Col Skinner & Major Wᵐ Fraser, of "Skinner's Irregular Horse".

MILITARY MEMOIR

OF

LIEUT.-COL. JAMES SKINNER, C.B.

FOR

MANY YEARS A DISTINGUISHED OFFICER COM-
MANDING A CORPS OF IRREGULAR CAVALRY
IN THE SERVICE OF THE H. E. I. C.

INTERSPERSED WITH

NOTICES OF SEVERAL OF THE PRINCIPAL PERSONAGES WHO
DISTINGUISHED THEMSELVES IN THE SERVICE
OF THE NATIVE POWERS IN INDIA.

BY J. BAILLIE FRASER, Esq.,

AUTHOR OF
"TRAVELS IN KHORASSAN, MESOPOTAMIA, AND KOURDISTAN," ETC. ETC.

IN TWO VOLUMES.
VOL. II.

1851.

CONTENTS.

CHAPTER XI.

CHAPTER XII.

CHAPTER XIII.

CHAPTER XIV.

CHAPTER XV.

CHAPTER XVI.

MEMOIRS,

&c. &c.

CHAPTER XI.

Holcar—His views—Predatory system—Negotiations with the British authorities—Threats—War—Monson's expedition—Capture of Tonk—Hinglaisghur—Advance by the Mookundra Pass—Retreat commenced by the same—Reach Kotah—Abandon their guns—Cross Chumbulee river—Reach Rampoorah—Joined by a reinforcement—Retreat continued—Cross the Bunas with severe loss—Major Sinclair killed — Reach Khooshalghur — Retreat, severely pressed, to Hindoun— Biana Pass—Troops thrown into disorder, disperse, and fly—Few reach Agra—Preparations for repairing the disaster—Holcar takes Muttra—Lord Lake marches to its relief—Tactics of the enemy—Holcar detaches infantry to Attack Dehlee—Gallant defence of that city—Battle of Deeg—Defeat and pursuit of Holcar—Capture of Deeg—Army breaks up—Termination of the campaign.

THE expedition and disastrous retreat of Colonel Monson is an event too painfully interesting to be dismissed with the imperfect notice taken of

VOL. II.   B

it by Skinner, though, from his thorough information, it must be, so far as it goes, perfectly
authentic.   It was, in fact, the first important inci-
dent of the new war, in which the principal subject of this memoir took a very active part; and
therefore, independently of its intrinsic interest,
we think it proper to explain to our readers how
it arose and was carried on.

The first Mahratta war, which was virtually
terminated in one campaign by the battle of
Laswarree in Hindostan, and that of Argaum
and the capture of Gawilghur in the Dekhan,
was waged only against Sindea and Bhounslah.   Holcar, whom Sindea had in vain invited to join the confederacy, held aloof, though
he had vaguely promised assistance.   His conduct, as Mr. Grant Duff observes, was precisely
that of a cautious, designing Mahratta.   Dread-
ing as he did the power and hereditary enmity
of Sindea, he was by no means ill-pleased at the
chance of his rival being somewhat crippled by
a collision with the British; and even should they
be worsted, and the advantage remain with that
rival, his own power would be all the more entire
and fit to resist whatever might come upon him,
by keeping clear of the fray.   Like his father and

his whole family, he leant to the predatory rather than the regular system of making war, and trusted that, by avoiding fair fighting and laying waste the country round his enemy, he should cripple him more effectually than by assailing him with regular infantry and cannon.

This impression may account for the somewhat daring hope he must have entertained of being able, single-handed, to accomplish what both Sindea and Bhounslah could not effect together, and not only to withstand, but to defeat the power which had prostrated them in a single campaign. But he did not despise assistance. On the contrary, he sought it, on grounds of mutual interest, from the Rajepoots, the Jhats, the Rohillas, and the Sikhs; and, though last not least, from Ameer Khan, the Pindarree chief, who, indeed, may be regarded as one of his own dependants. He even attempted to persuade Sindea to renew the struggle, and though fruitlessly at the time, either Sindea or his ministers appear to have left the matter open so far as to be able to act as circumstances should determine, though they communicated the overture to the British authorities at the time.

There, indeed, had long been suspicions of Holcar, though it would have been inconvenient to bring matters to a rupture while their hands were otherwise full. He had made inroads on districts they regarded as under British protection, and had ruined Malwa by enormous exactions, levied on a system of cruel force, as yet unheard of save by barbarians in a plundering inroad. From the town of Mundissore, the emporium of commerce from all quarters, he forced, by treachery and torture, immense sums. No trifle was too slight, no merchandize too cumbrous; even furniture and women's ornaments were snatched to make up the sum, which exceeded from this devoted town alone a million sterling.* He was roused from his system of robbery, by accounts of the incredible course of victory by which the English had delivered Hindostan, and he now resolved to act, though still maintaining the tone of negociation. His letters, indeed, were of a very inconsistent character; at one time breathing threats and insult, at another protesting that his friendship was sincere and lasting. As he moved towards Rajepootanah he wrote to Lord Lake, requesting him to retire towards Agra, "as his near approach to his victorious army might lead

* Sir John Malcolm's "Central India."

to unpleasant circumstances;" and almost in his next he declares that the General shall never have from him any language but that of friendship; but if any other than friendly words should come *from* him, then he, Holcar, would be helpless. To General Wellesley he wrote, threatening that, though unable to face his guns, " countries of many hundred côs shall be overrun, he (Lake) shall not have leisure to breathe for a moment, and calamity will fall on lakhs of human beings by a continued war, in which my army will overwhelm all like the waves of the sea."

Questions and negotiations succeeded each other, and the savage murder of his three English officers, Tod, Ryan, and Vickers, aggravated the growing quarrel. It was obvious that further temporizing was but playing the enemy's game, and that, unless something were speedily done, Rajepootanah would be rendered a waste, like northern Malwa. The inevitable war was commenced, and the first measure taken was that of the celebrated expedition under Colonel Monson, which was sent on the 23rd of April to drive Holcar from the territory of Jeypore. This was soon effected, Holcar rapidly retired to the southward as the detachment approached; and on Lord Lake making a demonstration with the rest of the army, he continued his route across the Chumbul, and regained his own frontier.

On the 6th of May, the fort of Tonk Rampoorah was gallantly stormed by Lieutenant-Colonel Don: on which Lord Lake sent the main army back to cantonments, leaving Colonel Monson with five battalions of native infantry, and about 3,000 irregular horse, under Lieutenant Lucan and Bappoojee Sindea, to keep Holcar in check. It had been intended that a detachment to co-operate with Colonel Monson should be sent from Guzerat under Colonel Murray; but the junction never took place. Trusting to this, however, it appears Colonel Monson entered Holcar's country by the Mookundra pass to the southward of Kotah, took the strong hill-fort of Hinglaisghur by escalade, a most gallant and brilliant exploit, and advanced fifty miles south of the pass, into Malwa, where he expected to communicate with Murray; then, hearing that Holcar had recrossed the Chumbul, probably on hearing of General Lake's return to quarters, the Colonel made a forward movement to meet and fight him. But shortness of provisions alarmed him; and having now learned from Colonel Murray, that, instead

of advancing to effect a junction, he meant to fall
back upon the Myhie river, Monson resolved also
to retire backwards by the Mookundra pass.

On the 8th of July, this disastrous retreat commenced. The baggage and stores were sent off
at four in the morning, while Monson remained
in order of battle, on the ground of his encampment, till half-past nine. No enemy appearing,
he commenced his march, leaving the irregular
cavalry behind, with orders to follow in half an
hour, and bring intimation of what the enemy
was about. The detachment had marched only
six côs, when intelligence came that the irregular
cavalry had been attacked and defeated by Holcar's horse, and while orders were given for the
troops to form and support the rear-guard, Bappoojee Sindea rode up to say that the force had
been cut up, and Lieutenant Lucan with the
other officers, after a brave defence, were wounded
and made prisoners. On this, the order was
countermanded as useless, and the march was
continued to Sonârâ which the baggage had
already reached. On the following morning,
the 9th, the army moved again, and reached
the Mookundra pass the same day at noon.

On the morning of the 10th, a large body of

the enemy's cavalry made their appearance, and increased in numbers until noon of the following day, when Holcar summoned the detachment to surrender their arms. This being contemptuously refused, he divided his force into three bodies, with which he vigorously attacked the British in front and flanks. But he was gallantly and successfully repulsed in every effort; till, at the approach of night, he drew off some three miles distance, intending, as was supposed, to attack, with the aid of his infantry and guns, which had now come up.

Monson, not deeming his post tenable against such a force, and fearing to have his retreat cut off, resolved to march and reach Kotah in two days, much harassed by unfavourable weather and the flooded state of the country; but the men behaved well, repeatedly repulsing the enemy with material loss, while suffering little themselves.

At Kotah, Zalim Sing declined to admit the troops within the walls; and, it is said, would not supply them with provisions of which they were much in want. Colonel Tod denies that, on the part of Zalim Sing, and asserts, that he not only offered to furnish them with food, but *did* send troops to assist and protect their rear, when a brave chief (of Coelah) and many of his party were slain.* However this may be, Monson continued his route towards the Gaumuch ford, a distance of only seven miles; but which, from the depth of the mud and incessant rain, took a whole night to accomplish; and when they did reach it, the rivulet was too much swollen to be fordable. They therefore halted here, not only until it should fall, but to procure a supply of provisions from the neighbouring village of Puttun. On the 15th, the march was resumed; but the guns sunk so deep in the mud that they could not be extricated, and were therefore rendered useless, and abandoned; but they were recommended to the care of the Rajah of Boondee, who remained stanch to his engagements, in the face of Holcar.

On the 17th, the troops reached the Chumbulee rivulet, which was not fordable; but the artillerymen were crossed the next day on elephants, with orders to proceed to Rampoorah. For nearly ten days was the gradual passage of the detachment effected by elephants and rafts, and some by a "ford" lower down, during which time they were

* Tod's " Rajepootanah," vol. ii. p. 549.

constantly harassed by attacks of the enemy, and
still more distressed by privations of all sorts;
many of the men were drowned in crossing the
Chumbulee, and many of the poor sepoys had to
deplore the loss of their wives or children, left,
often necessarily, on the opposite banks till the
last, and then murdered within sight of their
husbands by the Bheels from the neighbouring
hills, who were in Holcar's interest.   On the
21st, Captain Odonnel destroyed a camp of the
enemy's, and took several camels and horses; and
as the troops were crossing on the 24th, Colonel
Monson, with only 700 men, maintained a sharp
contest with the enemy's cavalry, who withdrew
at sunset with considerable loss, the British only
losing twenty in killed and wounded.

It was the 27th of July before Colonel Monson
and all the troops arrived at Rampoorah, which
they reached in a most exhausted state.   Here,
however, the Colonel had the satisfaction of being
joined by two battalions of sepoys, with four
6-pounders and two howitzers, and a body of
irregular horse, under Major Frith, with a supply
of grain from Agra, all sent by General Lake, on
hearing of the situation of the detachment at the
Mookundra pass.   Yet, notwithstanding this re-

lief, and all that could be procured at Rampoorah, the Colonel resolved to pursue his march to Khooshalghur, where he expected to find a further reinforcement of six of Sindea's battalions, with twenty-one guns. Leaving, therefore, a strong garrison at Rampoorah with the field-pieces, the detachment, now consisting of five battalions of Bengal sepoys with the two howitzers, reached the Bunas river at daybreak on the 22nd of August. But it was not fordable, and three boats having been found, one of the battalions was sent across by their means with the treasure, with orders to proceed to Khooshalghur.

Next morning the enemy appeared, and pitched their camp about four miles distant from the British detachment. On the morning of the 24th, the river having fallen, Monson began to transport across his baggage. The greater part of this, along with four battalions, had crossed, and the 2nd battalion of the 2nd Bengal sepoys, who, under command of Major James Sinclair, had been left as a rear-guard, were preparing to follow with the piquets, as soon as the rest should have passed, when the enemy, many of whose cavalry had by this time crossed above and below the British position, brought up their infantry and guns, and about four in the afternoon opened a heavy cannonade on the small body of English still on that side the river.

They were led to the charge by the gallant Major Sinclair, and drove the enemy from their guns as fast as they formed in battery against them. But fresh troops poured in, and fresh batteries showered grape upon them, until, thinned and overpowered, they were forced to retreat, and the remnant of this gallant band crossed the river under the fire of the battalions on the other side, who came down to the bank to check the enemy. But the loss was calamitous; thirteen European officers, with their brave commander, having fallen in this desperate charge. The whole detachment, indeed, suffered severely; and the enemy pressing his advantage, Monson was forced to abandon his baggage, and fly to Khooshalghur, which he reached on the night of the 25th of August, after repulsing several desultory attacks of the enemy's cavalry.

At this place, they found that Sedasheo Bhow, who had been sent to their assistance, intended, as a preliminary in the way of his vocation, to levy a contribution on the town of Khooshalghur, which Captain Nichols, who had escorted the treasure thither, resolved to prevent. The Bhow, enraged, opened his guns upon the place, and then attempted an attack with his infantry; but both were repulsed by Captain Nichols, with a severe loss to the Mahrattas.

On the morning of the 26th, the whole of the enemy's cavalry encamped in separate bodies around the detachment. But the most disheartening circumstance in their case, was the discovery of a correspondence between some of the native officers and the enemy, and, though immediate measures were adopted to check the mischief, two companies of infantry and a large proportion of the irregular cavalry deserted to the enemy. On the same day Monson quitted the fort, having spiked the remaining howitzer, and forming his troops into an oblong square, resumed his march. During that night and the following day, the enemy's cavalry, supported by some guns, attempted, but unsuccessfully, to penetrate the square. On the night of the 27th, they took possession of the ruined fort of Hindoun, and at one o'clock next morning continued their retreat towards Agra. They had no sooner cleared the ravines near Hindoun, however, than a desperate charge, in three separate bodies, was made upon

them by the enemy's horse; but the sepoys re-
serving their fire till the enemy had come up
almost to the bayonet points, it told with great
effect, and they fled in all directions.   At sunset
on the 28th, they reached the Biana pass, where,
from the exhausted and suffering condition of the
troops, Colonel Monson halted, and would have
passed the night; but the enemy brought up his
guns, and opened so galling a fire that he was
forced to prosecute the retreat, which was continued to the town of Biana.   But the night was
dark, the camp followers and baggage got mixed
with the line, the troops were thrown into inex-
tricable confusion, order could no more be restored, the troops fairly broke and fled; and such
as escaped the straggling parties of the enemy—
for there was no further regular attack—made
their way to Agra, which they reached, in flying
and detached groups, on the 31st of August.

Such was the disastrous retreat from Mookundra, the result of which, though certainly occasioned in some degree by unavoidable misfortunes
and the untowardness of the season for military
operations, cannot, we think, be viewed by those
who know the sepoys, as free from mistakes,
which a more intimate knowledge of that gallant

body of men might have avoided. And there is the greater reason for believing this, from the fact, recorded by Skinner himself, of a serjeant having marched into Agra with about 1,500 of the sepoys, whom he and some native officers had rallied and collected into a body when the flight took place.

To remedy so serious a disaster, and to prepare, not only to repulse a victorious enemy, but to repress the rebellious spirit of those already subdued, yet still discontented, became now an imperative obligation; and the courage and resources of the Commander-in-chief were equal to the emergency. Even the cruel dispositions of the tyrant turned to his own loss, for the mutilated sepoys who escaped his hands roused the indignation of their brethren, and not only excited a spirit of retaliation, but caused even deserters to flock again to their colours. But while the various arrangements were in progress, Holcar, with 60,000 horse of all sorts, 15,000 infantry, and 192 guns, advanced rapidly to Muttra, which was abandoned at his approach. Parties of his horse even crossed the Jumna, but were soon driven back, and on the 1st of October, Lord Lake, with his army, marched from Secundra, where it had

been assembled to attack Holcar's camp at Muttra. But that chief had no intention whatever of
making a stand. He fled immediately at the first
discharge of a galloper gun; and though many
efforts were made to surprise his camp, the vigi-
lance of fear and habitual predatory precaution
prevented his sustaining any serious loss.

"At an early hour on the 10th," says Major
Thorn, "another attempt was made to bring the
enemy to an engagement, for which purpose the
infantry moved in the same direction as before,
whilst the cavalry made a greater circuit to the
right to cut off their retreat; but they were so
much on their guard since the last affair, that
they had posts out in all directions, who by firing
matchlocks and burning lights gave the signal of
alarm. Our cavalry formed in two lines, moved
in columns of half regiments at regular intervals.
In this order, we swept clear the whole plain
where the enemy were encamped, at a full gallop;
but we could not succeed in our endeavour. to
charge them, for they scampered off in all directions, dispersing as usual. When we halted, they
did the same, rallied, and stood gazing at us, and
when we turned our backs to return home, they
dashed on, attacking our rear and flanks, firing

long shots from their matchlocks, while those who were armed with spears and tulwars, flourished their weapons, making at the same time a noise like jackalls, by way of bravado. On this occasion, about thirty of the enemy were killed, and several made prisoners, who naturally enough expected to meet with the most severe treatment, in retaliation for the perfidious cruelties committed by the master, of whom they gave this curious account, that he was the first to run away. Instead, however, of that vengeance which these men looked for at our hands, they received each a rupee by order of their general, who dismissed them with this message to their chief, that none but cowards treated their prisoners with cruelty."

The unavoidable delay of our army at Muttra had, however, afforded to Holcar an opportunity of striking a blow, which, if successful, might have had serious consequences. This was no less than, by a *coup-de-main*, to surprise Dehlee, and get possession of the emperor's person, to which, fallen as he was, public opinion in Hindostan still attached much of veneration and traditional importance. For this purpose the whole of his infantry and artillery were detached from his army, under command of an adopted son, Hurnaut, and on the

8th of October commenced their attack upon the
Moghul capital.   Colonel Ochterlony, the British
resident at the emperor's court, with his usual
sagacity, had suspected this intention of Holcar,
from the time he reached Khooshalghur, and had
prudently called in Colonel Burn and his detachment from Seharunpore, a battalion, late of
Sindea's, under Major Harriot, from Rohtuck,
and one of Nujeebs, under Lieutenant Birch,
from Paneeput; and to these were added, about
1,200 matchlock-men of various sorts, and four
companies of the 17th regiment.   But this force,
after all, amounted only to two battalions and
four companies of sepoys, about 800 Telingas
of Sindea's, two corps of irregular cavalry, and
Birch's Nujeebs, with the matchlock-men.   Of
these troops one-third, or 800 of the regular
sepoys, were required by the resident in the
palace itself, to guard the emperor's person.   One
of the corps of irregular horse went over to the
enemy at his approach; the second, being found
utterly useless, and not to be depended on, was
sent off across the Jumna into the Doab, and the
Nujeebs mutinied on pretence of want of pay,
though only fourteen days' pay was due to them.
The mutiny, indeed, was suppressed; some were

blown from a gun, others were flogged; but the corps was annihilated. The other corps remained faithful to their duty. And to the honour of all be it recorded, that not another desertion occurred during the whole of this most remarkable and arduous defence.

This, with but few and very insufficient artillery, was, as will be admitted, a most inadequate garrison for a city seven miles in circumference, with no works, save an old ruinous wall of the worst description of masonry—in many places, without a parapet fit to mount a gun upon, or able to stand the shock of one if fired — without a ditch, and surrounded on all sides by ruins and cover, up to the very foot of the wall; add to this, a most turbulent and idle-disposed population, and it will not be denied that its defenders had no enviable task in having to protect it against an army of 15,000 regular infantry with nearly 200 guns, and backed by 60,000 horse.

The question was, whether, with such inadequate means, the defence should be limited to the fort or palace, abandoning the city to its fate? But Colonel Burn, who, as senior officer, had assumed the command, considering the evil effect it would have upon the British name were the city given up, resolved, on his own responsibility, to defend both as long as possible.

Although the enemy did not take this brave garrison unaware, there was yet but scanty time to make the needful arrangements: but redoubts were erected at the Ajmere and Toorkoman gates, and some part of the rampart was strengthened for guns. On the 7th, Holcar's horse made their appearance, and after an attempt at reconnoitering and driving them back, on the part of Lieutenant Rose, Captain Carnegie, and Lieutenant Hunter, which was defeated by the cowardice of the irregular cavalry, the troops retired within the walls. Next day, the 8th, the enemy's infantry and artillery approached in force, and commenced a heavy cannonade upon the southeast angle of the city wall: and, though compelled to withdraw by the fire from the garrison, some thirty or forty feet of the parapet had fallen from the concussion of its own guns, or been levelled by the enemy's shot. During the night, breaching batteries were erected, which totally destroyed the parapet and made partial breaches in the wall: and, as it was probably here the first attempt would be made, it was resolved to check the enemy's progress by a sally. This did not,

however, take place until the 10th, when Lieutenant John Rose,* aide-de-camp to Colonel Burn,
with 200 sepoys, 150 Nujeebs, a reserve of fifty
men and a 6-pounder, moved out to the attack.
It was eminently successful; they gained the battery, spiked the guns, and retreated with very
little loss, leaving the enemy fighting each other
in the confusion and the darkness.

A battery of two heavy guns had been erected
the same day by Captain Keating; and, when the
enemy again opened their guns from the battery
which had been stormed, both it and the more
distant ones were silenced by the Captain's well-
directed fire. On this the enemy drew off,
and commenced operations on the southern face
of the city, and all within the walls remained
watching with vigilant anxiety for the next
attack. Their heaviest guns were now placed
opposite the curtain between the Toorkoman and
Ajmere gates, under cover of some gardens and
ruins. A breach was soon effected; but a work
thrown up inside, cutting off the breached part,
rendered that of no use to them, and the men
worked hard and willingly to accomplish this important operation.

* Now Major-General Sir John Rose, K.C.B.

On the 14th, at daybreak, the enemy's guns opened from every direction, and, under cover of this cannonade, an escalade by infantry in large numbers was tried at the Lahore gate; but they were driven back with much loss in men, and all their ladders. Unfortunately, Lieut. Simpson, of the 17th regiment, was killed by a cannon-shot. After this, no further desperate attack was attempted. A show was made at the Cashmere gate, but, before the morning of the 15th, the enemy's whole force had moved off, and at daybreak their rear-guard was seen at a distance by the weary garrison, who for eight days and nights had been incessantly but cheerfully struggling to save the place. Such is a short narrative of the chief events of this memorable defence; but it is not easy to convey an idea of the persevering exertions by which success was attained. The fatigue suffered by both men and officers could only be equalled by the cheerful patience with which it was borne. And when we consider not only the defenceless condition in which this small body of men was exposed to the assault of an organized and well-supplied multitude, but the state of feeling in the country from the late triumph of that enemy, and the disastrous defeat

so recently sustained, it may give some idea
of what the sepoy really is, and what he will do
when led by officers whom he loves and con-
fides in.   And little often is the trifle which will
cheer them to extra toil and extra danger.   A
small allowance of sweetmeats, in addition to
their daily provisions—for they had no time to
cook food—was found on this occasion to have
the happiest effect upon the men, and half a
month's pay of gratuity, when the enemy was
repulsed, rendered them grateful and happy.
Kindness and firmness on the part of their officer,
and a full reliance on his judgment, will kindle
the zeal and devotion of the sepoy to any exertion.   Both Colonel Ochterlony and Colonel Burn
knew them well, and richly did their country
reap the fruits of their knowledge, and of their
intrepid firmness, in the siege of Dehlee.

We do not pretend to give an account of the
war, and though we cannot refrain from advert-
ing at some length to remarkable feats of gallantry, our purpose in these notes is merely to
follow the course of Colonel Skinner's career, and
to give so much of the general current events
as may serve to explain and illustrate it.   We
therefore pass over the rapid movements which

took place on either side by the contending parties, and in which it will be seen that Skinner had his share. Even the celebrated battle of Deeg must not detain us long, although there, in spite of a position deemed impregnable, and chosen by his own generals, Holcar, in one morning's work, lost nearly a hundred of his guns, his two best commanders, more than 2,000 of his infantry, with the field, and his character for good fortune. But we must drop one word of regret for the loss of the gallant General Fraser, and many other brave officers, for the field was not won without the loss of 643 killed and wounded, of whom five officers were among the first, and seventeen among the second list. Nor can it be uninteresting to mention that, among the captured artillery, Colonel Monson found fourteen of his own guns, and several ammunition tumbrils, lost during his unfortunate retreat.

Four days after this brilliant success, Holcar received another check to his pride, in being surprised in his camp, in spite of his boasted alertness. After a rapid and destructive run through the Doab, burning, plundering, and destroying, Holcar came to Futtehghur, and had encamped there in safety, as he believed, being thirty-six miles ahead of the pursuing force. But General Lake, by a forced night march, and led by excellent intelligence, reached the outskirts of the enemy's camp just as day was breaking, on the morning of the 17th. Holcar had heard, just the evening before, at a nautch, the news of the battle of Deeg, but he said nothing to his chiefs, and retired to his tents as usual. An artillery tumbril blew up towards morning in the British line of march, and started him; but they told him it was the morning gun from Futtehghur, and he believed it. Even when the firing commenced, such confidence had he in his spies, that he could not believe it was Lord Lake, as they told him. All seemed to combine to lull his usual acuteness to sleep. The men, wrapt in their blankets, were still sleeping by their piqueted horses, when they were roused by showers of grape; and before those who had not been sent to their last slumber could rise and look about them, the King's 8th Light Dragoons were amongst them, cutting them down right and left; the other regiments soon galloped up and did the same, so that the plain was soon covered with the bodies of the dead.

Holcar, too late convinced, mounted his horse, and never stopped till he was eighteen miles dis-

tant, on the road to Mynpooree. The rest, left
to themselves, dispersed or were cut up. Some,
whose horses were even more jaded than ours, by
their desperate marches, climbed into the mango
trees, and thus escaped for the time. But some of
them, unable to resist firing on the dragoons as
they passed, were discovered and shot among the
branches. For ten miles did the pursuit continue,
and as the night march was good fifty-eight miles,
the cavalry had thus ridden over a space of seventy
miles in twenty-four hours, an almost unparalleled
feat, especially after a most harassing march of 350
miles within the previous fortnight.* The loss
of the British was trifling—scarce twenty men.
That of Holcar, severe in itself, being not less than
3,000 men upon the ground, was infinitely more
so from its consequences. By desertions and dis-
persions, his force, on that morning reckoned at
60,000 men, was so reduced that he never mustered half that number again, and, what was still
worse, he lost his *nam*, his prestige, which, from
his first successes, had risen high in Hindostan.

Among other fortunate consequences of this

---

* It was the training in that and such marches that
enabled both horse and man to perform such extraordinary
feats, and even to beat Holcar at his own tactics.

victory, was the saving of the European civilians and merchants, who, abandoning the open cantonment, had taken refuge in the fort. There they defended themselves bravely, but could not have long held out; and happy were the almost despairing gentlemen of Futtehpore and Mynpooree, when the yellow coats of " Skinner's horse " made their appearance as their deliverers.

There yet remained one blow to complete the fall of Holcar, and that was the capture of the strong fortress of Deeg. This, as well as Bhurtpore, was the stronghold of the Jhats, and the Rajah of the latter place, so well known in Indian warfare, had been the dependant rather than the ally of Holcar ever since the rise of that chieftain to power. The loss of his guns and infantry, and his subsequent defeat near Futtehghur, had reduced him to a change of condition; he had now become rather dependant on the Rajah, and the fortress of Deeg was manned by their joint forces: for their interests were now too closely united for one to fall without bringing down the other.

On the 13th of December, the batteries opened against Deeg; on the 23rd, the breach was stormed in the usual gallant and irresistible way; and though the enemy's men, particularly the

Golunduz, or artillerists, fought with the most resolute bravery, never quitting their guns till bayoneted at them to a man, and though a fierce and most bloody conflict was maintained through-out the whole of this most arduous day, by two o'clock of the following morning, the town, the shahbourg, and outworks, with all their guns, were in possession of the British. The garrison of the inner fort, dispirited and hopeless, were seen streaming off in parties during that day; and on the morning of Christmas 1804, both town and fort, with all the remaining artillery of Holcar, his stores of grain and some treasure, remained in the hands of the besiegers.

It falls not in with our duty or our plan, to touch upon the seige of Bhurtpore, with its four most gallant though disastrous assaults. Heavy and sad as was the loss of life before its ill-omened walls, the sacrifice was not altogether in vain : for it convinced the Rajah of his own impotence to resist a power which had pulled down princes so much his superior, and which must soon exhaust his own resources and destroy him. And though "Bhurtpore" continued for long to be a taunt and a reproach to us in Upper India, those who knew us best were well aware that a timely submission alone saved the Jhat prince from the fate of his allies. As for Holcar, baffled, beaten, and dishonoured, stripped of his guns and his troops, the fortresses of his family in our hands, with scarce a home to fly to, this free-booter who crossed the Chumbul with 70,000 men and 200 guns, breathing arrogant threats of ruin and extermination to the British, in less than ten short months fled before that power, and re-crossed that river a wandering fugitive with scarce 8,000 horse and 4,000 or 5,000 infantry.

On the 21st of April, the army broke up from before Bhurtpore, and crossing the Chumbul, made a progress towards Bundelcund, forming a junction with the division, which was acting in that quarter and arranging treaties with the chiefs. They returned from thence in May, and in the beginning of June were distributed in quarters for the rainy season along the west side of the Jumna.

Thus terminated these two bright and rapid campaigns, which for the magnitude of the effects they accomplished, the brilliant succession of exploits performed in them, and the daring gal-lantry and intrepid resolution they exhibited, have never perhaps been surpassed. In less than two years, three powerful princes, elated with a long career of success, besides many minor chiefs, the aggregate of whose forces was at least 400,000 men, with 500 guns; possessed of innumerable strongholds, many of which were held to be impregnable, were completely humbled, their armies scattered, their guns captured, and their fortresses stormed and taken. And this by a force which, taking natives and Europeans together, never exceeded in number a tenth part of their adversaries. Nor were these successes gained over feeble enemies, as the heavy lists of killed and wounded will sufficiently testify; but neither their numbers nor their courage could avail against the steady discipline and regulated valour of British soldiers. Honour, then, to the brave and skilful men who led, and to the gallant troops, native as well as English, who under such guidance achieved such deeds! The indomitable courage of British soldiers is too well known to require panegyric; but those who do not know the Indian sepoy should be made aware how well he has vindicated his claim to stand beside his European comrade, and how little he will yield to him in the hour of need, in zeal, in intrepidity, and self-devotion.

CHAPTER XII.

COLONEL MONSON, says Skinner, was decoyed by Holcar to his capital; but he delayed attacking the Colonel until the setting-in of the rains, a sea-son as favourable to the operations of the Mah-rattas as it was adverse to the British, for the country of Malwa is so deep in the rains that wheel-carriages cannot move, a circumstance of which I believe the Colonel was not aware. Holcar also contrived to throw himself between Colonel Murray and Monson, and kept manœuvring about in hopes of an opportunity to strike some great blow. So bad was the information of the latter, that he was unable to effect a junction with Murray, who, thus unsupported and aware of the effect of the rains in that quarter, commenced his retreat to Baroda, without being able to apprise Colonel Monson of his intention.

Holcar, finding that he had thus gained his point, now turned upon Monson, and overtook him near Bhampoorah. The Colonel, who by this time had heard of the retreat of the Bombay detachment, resolved to fall back with his own corps by the Mookundra pass; but Holcar was too quick for him. He marched from Bhampoorah, leaving Lieutenant Lucan, who had command of all the Hindostanee horse, amounting to about 5,000 men, and some gallopers as a rear-guard; but · the detachment had not gone ten miles, when Holcar's advanced guard made its appearance before Lucan.

Had Lucan retreated at once, he might have saved himself; but he desired to make a name, and thought he might acquire it by making a brilliant charge before commencing his retreat; and so he might had his troops been stanch, but they were not. Bappoo Sindea, who commanded the greater portion, at the first movement went over to Holcar, and the Baraitch horse (whose master now enjoys a large jagheer), began to retreat at once without orders, so that poor Lucan was left with only his horse, amounting to 1,500, and two brave chiefs (never named by Government), Prithee Raj, a relative of the Bullumghur Rajah, with 500 horse, and the She-kâwat Rajah's son with 500 Rajepoots; these remained true to Lucan, and did honour to the field.

Lucan, after checking the advance party, which, by all accounts amounted to 5,000 horse, commenced his retreat, and continued in good order for six miles, unassisted by Gardiner's horse, who never came up or were heard of. Then, finding himself quite surrounded by Holcar's troops, he was forced to make a stand. In this situation he was charged by Wahud Allee Khan with an immense body of Bunjas, the best cavalry Holcar had; but he and the two chieftains stood the charge and repulsed the Bunjas with great slaughter, severely wounding Wahud Allee Khan. On this they cleared away a little, and Lucan again tried to retreat; but he was again charged from all quarters, and completely routed. He himself was wounded and made prisoner, and Prithee Raj and the Shekawut Rajah's son, with all their followers, were cut to pieces. The Baraitch Nawab was caught, wounded, and taken, and most of the cowardly fellows that left Lucan, on the enemy's first appearance, were overtaken and destroyed.

Monson had now gained the Mookundra pass, but thought fit to leave it for want of supplies. Had he continued in his position, he might have defied all the armies of Hindostan to drive him from it. But in making his retreat from Mookundra to Kotah, a distance of only sixteen côs, it came on to rain violently, and Monson lost almost all his guns, which were left sticking in the mud, together with all the tents. On his arrival at Kotah, Colonel Monson made application to the Rajah for provisions, and also for permission to leave two 12-pounder guns under his care. But Zalim Sing refused, declaring that he would neither furnish supplies nor take charge of the guns, unless he (the Colonel) would remain and attack Holcar; for, said he, if you march away, Holcar will take the guns, and punish me for assisting you with provisions.

Colonel Monson then left the guns to their fate, and commenced his march to Rampoorah, a fort near Tonke, which was garrisoned by British troops. This place he reached with great difficulty, being overtaken by Holcar in his retreat at the Bunas river which had risen, and could scarcely be crossed. At this place Major Sinclair, who, with a battalion of the 2nd regiment native infantry, was left as a rear-guard, was completely sacrificed. His conduct was noble, and shewed the natives of the country what British courage could do. He charged the enemy repeatedly, taking almost every gun that Holcar could bring against him; but troops pouring in upon him by thousands, and no assistance being to be had from Monson, he at length fell a victim, with all his party except one officer, in this zealous discharge of his duty. This gallant act of the sepoys, proving what they will do when properly led, will long be remembered both by Mahrattas and by Indians.

My corps having now been increased to 1,200 strong, and being joined by my brother who had

left the Begum's service, I was directed with all
haste to join Colonel S. Brown, who commanded
a large detachment of British troops at Muttra,
and who now was ordered to support Monson.   I
reached Muttra without trouble, and my men
were apparently quite stanch to the service.   I
had commenced crossing the Jumna, and got over
six rissalahs under charge of my brother, when
the rumours and alarm occasioned by Colonel
Monson's retreat, began to damp the spirits of
some of my men.   Immediately on understanding
this, I gave orders that 300 more should cross
and join my brother.   They saddled their horses
accordingly and went to the ghaut; but then,
believing themselves to be out of my sight, they
commenced their march towards Koorjah in the
Dooab. At this conjuncture I had with me 200 men,
100 being mounted on my own horses, the others
on horses of their own.   On the first I placed the
greatest reliance; but I was somewhat doubtful
of the attachment of the others; and seeing the
rascally conduct of the 300, I was somewhat at
a loss what conduct to pursue. Whilst medi-
tating on the subject I saw my Bargheers saddle,
which increased my uneasiness, for I feared they
were going to follow the example of the 300; but

from this apprehension my mind was soon relieved by their coming up in a body and requesting me to chastise the misconduct of the runaways, who were, they said, disgracing the character of the corps. To this I replied, that if they would swear upon their Koran to be faithful to me and to the service, I would then be proud to be their leader, and to this they immediately agreed. Lieutenant Boyd of the 15th Native Infantry, who, with a company of sepoys, had crossed to receive from me some treasure brought from Dehlee, was witness to this proceeding; and as soon as I was satisfied, I mounted my horse and desired my Bargheers to follow me, leaving the remainder in camp.

I overtook the runaways about a côs off, and when within 100 yards of them I ordered my yellow boys to halt, as I purposed to go forward and reason with them. When I got within hearing, the rissaldar, who was the leader of the deluded men, came up to me with four of his sowars. I tried to bring them to reason with mild words; but perceiving that these had no effect, I began to make use of abusive language and threats. On this the cowardly leader of the mutineers ordered one of his men to fire at me, and before I could draw either sword or pistol the man fired; but missing me, shot my horse dead on the spot through the head. My yellow boys seeing me fall, immediately gave a shout and charged them sword in hand, and with such good-will that about ninety of their number were cut up, the rest fled to a fort in the neighbourhood belonging to the Hatterass Rajah, who was not on friendly terms with the British Government. Of my party there were ten men killed, and several wounded.

Next morning I crossed the remaining portion of my party, and having joined Colonel Brown reported the occurrence to him. During the ten days we remained here, the detachment was much disheartened and perplexed by the alarming rumours and most painful objects coming in daily from the disastrous retreat of Monson. Poor Lucan had been tortured to death at Kotah, and two officers, left at Englaisghur by Monson, were beheaded by Hurnaut Sing, an adopted son of Holcar's; many others came into camp naked as they were born, and numbers of sepoys with their noses and ears cut off.* The three com-

* It would be a great injustice to suppose that such cruelties were common to all the Mahrattas,—such, in truth,

panies left at Englaisghur entered Holcar's service, and many more, who had from time to time
deserted during the retreat, also joined him, so
that he had now about 1,000 of the British sepoys
in his service. Holcar tried another attack upon
Monson near Khoosalghur, but was repulsed by
the British sepoys. Of the deserters, a great
number got into the square and were bayoneted.
Holcar's loss this day was severe.

Colonel Frith, who had been sent with his
corps of Hindostanee horse, joined at Rampoorah;
but on the first march from that place his men
went over to the enemy. Colonel Gardiner also
left the detachment when at Khoosalghur, and
went off to Jeypore, where he had formerly been on
service. Our situation thus became alarming, and
the more so from the discouragement occasioned
by the incessant arrivals of the victims of Monson's misfortune. Desertions from Muttra were

is not their real character. These barbarities were the
effects of Holcar's peculiar disposition, which was jealous
and revengeful in the extreme. His mutilations of the sepoys
appears to have been from their refusal to enter his service;
a circumstance which not only tends greatly to the credit and
high character of those who endured it, but tends to lessen
the culpability of those who took the other alternative, and
did enter his service.

numerous, and, in fact, the greatest confusion I ever witnessed prevailed amongst the troops there.

The detachment consisted of five battalions of sepoys, a regiment of regular cavalry, 900 of my horse, and twenty pieces of cannon, with three lakhs of Brinjarrahs, loaded with provisions sufficient to last the detachment for several months. However, a council of war was held to decide whether the detachment was to fall back on Agra, or to stand out at Muttra. The officers commanding corps, namely, Colonel Ball, Colonel Toone, Major Hammond, Major Burrel, and Colonel Brown, were summoned to head-quarters. I, also, was honoured by a call, but did not vote. Colonels Brown, Ball, and Toone, were for falling back to Agra, Burrel and Hammond of the 2nd for standing fast at Muttra.

Next evening, about sunset, the detachment all of a sudden paraded, and in an hour after, marched off to Agra, leaving tents and almost everything behind. Being pitched at some distance, I knew nothing of all this, until my brother, who was for piquet, proceeding with 200 men to his post about an hour after they had gone, was surprised to find no piquet party; my men who were on duty, fifty in number, having gone off to

Bhurtpore, followed by the jemadar with his party of regulars. On this he returned to me with the information that the army had gone off. I instantly saddled, and, striking my tents, formed my men in two columns with the two 6-pounders. About three hours after the detachment had left us I commenced my march, and soon found out the road they had taken, by the followers. Of the enemy I saw nothing, and joined the main body within two côs of Gowghaut.

Desiring my brother to remain in rear of the 1st cavalry, I went up to the commanding officer and told him all the circumstances, when he said he would halt at Gowghaut. The best of the business was, that Holcar was running off one way, while we were going another; and when we arrived at Gowghaut the troops were so much knocked up and straggling, that I do not believe any regiment could number twenty men under their colours. The officers had lost almost everything they possessed; and such was our fright and confusion, that had the detachment met with 1,000 resolute men of the enemy, we should have made a worse business of it than Monson's. My hircarrahs brought me intelligence that Holcar, who had encamped at Futtehpore Seekree, had fled that night towards Bhurtpore, believing that the detachment was coming to surprise him; while Colonel Burn's hircarrahs, on the other hand, brought him information that Holcar's brigade had arrived at Futtehpore—though they were not within 100 côs of that place—and that he meant to push on for Gowghaut to cut off our retreat. It was this that made the Colonel push on towards Agra in such a hurry, and such was his alarm that he would not stop at Gowghaut, but pushed on to Agra, where we took shelter under the fort, and so greatly was the character of the British troops degraded in the native eyes by this behaviour, that the very thieves pelted us all night with stones.*

In this position we remained for three days,

---

* Nothing can be more striking, or more instructive, than Skinner's account of these disgraceful events : showing, as it does, the naked truth, stripped of the conventional form of official despatches ; illustrating, too, as it so forcibly does, the demoralizing effect of even a small reverse ; and the importance, in Indian warfare, of holding it a maxim at all times rather to dare the worst, and die upon the ground, if necessary, than retreat in face of an enemy. Retreat is almost always more disastrous than defeat; and the military history of our Indian empire abounds in instances where success has attended a resolute resistance even against overwhelming numbers.

witnessing the most horrible cruelties performed by Holcar on Monson's soldiers. The 1,000 men, who had gone over to him in the retreat, had begun to desert back to us from Futtehpore, and Holcar, in order to make an example that should deter the rest from following their example, cut off the noses, ears, and right hands from 200 of them. This act of cruelty was the saving of us, for our sepoys, who had been deserting by hundreds, seeing these poor mutilated wretches coming in daily, ceased at once to leave their regiments. At length, after all the surviving officers had come in, I saw about 1,500 men march in to camp with colours flying under command of a sergeant, with a great number of soobahdars and jemadars of native corps. These heroes had kept their ground after all the officers had left them. The poor sergeant was never noticed. This body of men had made good their way, pursued by Holcar's cavalry, to within eight côs of Agra.

This was the termination of both retreats; for Colonel Macan now arrived and took command of this unfortunate detachment, which had run all the way from Muttra to Agra without seeing an enemy. Colonel Macan marched us to Secundra, and brought the whole force into order: regular piquets were thrown out and rounds observed; cavalry regiments poured in every day, and Lord Lake, with the Europeans, was expected to arrive from Cawnpore.   Holcar took possession of Muttra, assembled all his troops, and sent his brigade, under command of Harnaut, to attack Dehlee. The 2nd cavalry was reported by its commanding officer " refused to cross."   Colonel Macan went to the spot determined to shoot the first man who should refuse.   The regiment was ordered to parade, and move to the ghaut.   The Colonel then ordered the first troop to cross, when not a man refused, and it was found out that they had never got orders to do so.   Colonel Gordon was immediately removed, and a new commander appointed.   Had there been a few more Macans in the service, many a disgraceful thing might have been avoided.

Holcar's horse now made their appearance, and daily skirmishes regularly took place.   Had Colonel Macan possessed full powers, we should soon have destroyed Holcar, who now was enjoying himself at Muttra, revelling in the *lall skraub** and brandy of the stores left there by the detachment.   He gave himself up to nautching and all

* Claret.

sorts of voluptuousness, which, luckily for us, had such an effect upon his health that he could not move from his bed. At Muttra he remained a month, issuing purwannahs and sending collectors to the Doab, and bestowing purgunnahs in jagheer to everybody who would join him. Among the rest he sent a man named Allahmeer, with 100 horsemen to Major Wood, who commanded the fort of Alleeghur, with a demand to deliver up the fort to him immediately, or he would not spare a man. The Major, although he had a battalion and provisions for several months in the fort, was so much alarmed at this threat, that he actually promised to give up the fort in fifteen days, and wrote off to Lord Lake, who by this time had arrived at Mynpooree with all the European troops, informing him of the treaty he thus had made with Holcar's soobah. I need not state his lordship's answer—the world will easily judge of its nature.

In the mean time, his lordship was approaching to Agra, where our army, increased by five regiments of native cavalry, was in excellent order, under Macan's command. At the commencement of Monson's retreat, we had in our pay about 20,000 Hindostanee horse in different places and under various officers. Since then, of them all, my corps was the only one which had remained stanch, the rest had all gone over to the enemy. Dehlee was now besieged by Holcar's brigade, while our army at Agra was looking out for Lake as earnestly as the Mussulmans, after a month's fast, look out for the new moon of the Eede. At length this new moon was seen on the 3rd September 1804, arriving at the tomb of Eelimâd-u-dowlut, which he reached with three regiments of dragoons, one of European foot, the famous 76th, and about fifteen or sixteen companies of sepoys.

My corps was now ordered to cross the river and join Lord Lake, which was done ; and next morning they were paraded, when his Excellency inspected them, and praising them highly for their fidelity, increased their pay ten rupees per horse ; and promised that they should have bread for life. He then ordered the European troops to cross, and directed Major Worsely, with the fifteen companies of sepoys to proceed to the Doab and drive all Holcar's collectors from thence, after which he was to rejoin the army at Muttra. His excellency then gave four galloper-guns to my corps, and directed me to join Major Worsely.

His lordship then joined the army, and commenced his march for Muttra on the 1st of October, attended by the whole of Holcar's horse, amounting, by the nearest calculation, to 40,000 men, who did their best to harass him on the way. But Holcar soon discovered that he had a very different person to deal with from Monson. Lord Lake kept the Jumna on his right, his baggage being between the river and the line, and reached Muttra in four or five marches, skirmishing all the way: Holcar now evincing great activity.

Major Worsely on his part took a round by Shekaobad, Zelasur, Coel, and Mahabun to Muttra: took several mud forts, hung up some of the soobahs who fought; and after a sharp and troublesome business, arrived in a few days at Hauseagunge opposite to Muttra. An able, steady, and active soldier, Major Worsely, received well-deserved praise for his zealous services, and was ordered to cross and take post in the town of Muttra with six companies of sepoys. The remaining part of his force with my horse were directed to stand fast at Hauseagunge, under the command of Major Munro; and as the Jumna was not fordable at this point, a

bridge of boats was ordered to be made ready
from the Hauseagunge ghaut to the town.   Lord
Lake had encamped on the west bank of the
river in the old Mahratta cantonments; and
Colonel Down with the reserve, consisting of
the remains of Monson's detachment, amounting
to about 2,000 sepoys, was pitched between the
army and the town.

All this time, Holcar was actively engaged in
cutting up small detachments coming with supplies
from Agra; so that in a few days provisions and
forage failed, and large bodies were forced to go
out for forage daily.   Day and night was the
camp surrounded with Holcar's horse, which were
no sooner attacked than they dispersed.   Several
mornings this was attempted with all the cavalry
and infantry; but the moment they saw us they
vanished, and no sooner had we returned to camp
and unsaddled, than there they were again sur-
rounding the camp, and quietly dismounting; not
less than from 10,000 to 20,000 of these horse
were thus constantly hovering about the camp,
and such became the scarcity, that three seers of
atta,* were selling for a rupee.

My corps was directed to work hard in the

* Coarse flour, the common food of the sepoys.

Doâb to remedy this scarcity, and get grain wherever it was to be found. I used to go out in the morning, plunder the villages, and send in whatever I could lay hold of; but it seldom exceeded the day's consumption, and the minds of the soldiers became so unsettled, and desertions so common again, that the troopers upon duty were found galloping over to the enemy from their posts: and in order to prevent such shameful desertions, Lord Lake was forced to place a sepoy with each trooper vidette, with orders to shoot the trooper if he should move towards the enemy. This state of anxiety and hardship continued for six days, and to add to it, alarming accounts arrived from Dehlee; the Resident entreating Lord Lake to come to his assistance with all despatch.

This his lordship was well disposed to do; but the army was just then waiting for the Brinjarrahs that were on their way from Cawnpore. They came unmolested until within two côs of Hattrass, when the Rajah stopped them, and said he would not permit them to go to Lord Lake; but would take the supplies himself. The Brinjarrahs at first refused; but at length being bribed they promised to give up the grain. When this information reached Lord Lake, he sent for me and asked whether I thought I could bring them away. I replied, that if his lordship would leave it to me, I would either bring off the supplies or lose my life in the attempt; on this, he shook me by the hand, and declared he never would forget my services.

I took my leave; and returning to camp collected all my hircarrahs, and as the Brinjarrahs were only eighteen côs distant, I laid a dak of hircarrahs, just to let me know when they should begin loading to go into the fort. The second day about midnight, information was brought me; and I immediately saddled and set off with all my horse, 1,200 in number. On reaching within a côs of them, I halted until my spies gave me information that they were all ready, and would move, if I did not prevent them. I left my brother with 800 men, and with 400 I dashed in amongst them, crying out that Lord Lake had sent me to their assistance. At first, they began throwing down their loads, declaring they would not go with me; but I ordered all who should attempt throwing their loads to be put to death; and several were accordingly killed. When they saw this, and found me determined, and perceiving my brother coming up with the large body, they gave in and called out, " Dohee, Lord Lake, kee; " so I ordered them to march towards Muttra, which they did.

By the time the sun had risen, I had got a côs off clear with my prize. But when the news reached the Rajah, he ordered all his horse to saddle and pursue me. I still pushed on; but when I had made two more côs, I ordered my brother with 600 men to go on with the convoy, and if any of the fellows should attempt throwing down their loads, to put them at once to death. I halted myself with the other 600 to show front to the Rajah, and in two hours afterwards I perceived his sowarree coming on. I now formed my party into two gholes, and made them a speech, telling them that I had promised Lord Lake either to bring in the Brinjarrahs or die. They were all stanch, and declared in reply they were ready to die with me. My brother had gained some four or five côs when the Rajah came up to me with, I think, about 1,200 men. I formed and showed front, when he sent a man to me to inquire who I was, and by whose authority I had taken the Brinjarrahs?

I gave my name accordingly, and said that I

had Lord Lake's *hookum,* which was the best in Hindostan. He sent in reply to order that I should immediately give up the Brinjarrahs, or he would instantly punish me. I replied that the Brinjarrahs and my head should go together, and that he had full liberty to do as he liked. He then sent on a few skirmishers in front, who fired at us; but some of my yellow boys soon sent their horses back without their riders. When the Rajah saw I was determined, and was not to be frightened, he asked me if I would take his vakeel to Lord Lake. To this, I replied that I would not take him now, lest the people might think that I had gained the Brinjarrahs by some false promise; but that if he would send him after, I would be his friend, and try to obtain his forgiveness. To this he agreed, and then marched back towards his fort.

For my part, I thanked the Almighty for my success, and joining my brother, arrived in the evening at Hauseagunge. The first person I saw was Major Worsely, who shook me warmly by the hand, and said that Lord Lake ought never to forget that day's work. I crossed and went to Lord Lake, who was at dinner; but hearing that I had arrived, immediately came out and asked me,

"Well, have you succeeded?" "Yes, my lord,"
was my reply, on which he also shook me by the
hand, and declared he never would forget me or
my corps. He then asked me to come in to dinner;
but I told him that having been eighteen hours on
horseback, I was pretty well knocked up; but
that I should wait on his lordship in the morning.

I returned to my tent accordingly, and ordered
for all my sowars a seer of sweetmeats each,
which, through Major Worsely's assistance, I got
from the town, and then ate my dinner. Next
morning, I called on his lordship and reported the
Brinjarrahs at 60,000 bullocks all loaded with
atta. On this, he again shook me by the hand,
and taking the sword he wore at his own waist,
presented it to me with 20,000 rupees. The Brinjarrah jemadars were also all handsomely rewarded
and ordered immediately to cross. These Brinjarrahs gave just seven days' supply to the army,
which enabled it to march, on the 12th of October,
to the relief of Dehlee, leaving Colonel Worsely
with his force to guard the town of Muttra.
Colonel Munro and my corps were detached
towards Anoopsheher in order to meet and escort
into camp a large convoy consisting of a lakh of
Brinjarrah bullocks loaded with atta, wheat, and

koonjah; and having met them, we accordingly proceeded with them to Dehlee, which place Lord Lake reached in eight or ten marches, much harassed all the way by Holcar's horse.

Four days previous to Lord Lake's arrival, Hurnaut had raised the siege of Dehlee, and retreated towards Deeg, through the Alwar pass, and then continued on towards Paneeput. His lordship could not follow for want of supplies, till our arrival, on the 27th of October, with the Brinjarrahs. Lord Lake then detached General Fraser in pursuit of Holcar's infantry, with all the infantry except the reserve under Colonel Down, which was ordered to cross the river. On the 29th, information was brought that Holcar had himself crossed at Koongepoorah to attack Colonel Burn's detachment, which had left Dehlee a few days previous to his lordship's arrival. This detachment consisted of one battalion of the 14th N. I. and three irregular battalions under Captain Harriott, formerly of the Mahratta service, and was proceeding to Seharunpore. On this the reserve was ordered to march towards Bhaugput, and my corps to go along with it, and on the 31st, Lord Lake, with all the cavalry, joined us, having crossed the Jumna at Bhaugput. By this time

Holcar had surrounded Burn's detachment in a small fort at Shamlee, after taking their baggage and bazaar; so that, no grain being to be had, they were living on sheep and bullocks.

Lord Lake reached Shamlee in two marches, and next morning Holcar showed a fine bold front, which rejoiced his lordship, as he now believed his enemy intended to stand.   He formed the cavalry in one line, and gave particular orders that no gallopers were to be opened on the enemy, but that the attack was to be made sword in hand. Whilst we were forming, however, a body of Holcar's horse made a false attack upon our right, on which the gallopers were instantly fired; and proved just the signal for Holcar to disperse, and so effectually was this done, that in less than an hour the whole of that immense body was out of sight.   We trotted after them for about four miles; but it was all to no purpose—we had to return without effecting anything, and his lordship was so enraged at the disappointment, that he swore he would deprive these regiments of their galloper guns.

We encamped near the town, which was given up to plunder,* and Colonel Burn received high

* The inhabitants of Shamlee deserved this well; for,

praise for his gallant defence of the position. After a day's halt, we commenced our march to Meerut, which was the road taken by Holcar; but when near Katowlee, we heard that he was still at that place, endeavouring to persuade the Begum Sumroo to join him, which she was not disinclined to do. On this Lord Lake turned his course towards Katowlee, and when six côs distant, he sent me off with my yellow troop to discover if he were there still. I had not gone two côs when I met 500 of his sowars, who were coming for information respecting our movements; and who immediately sent off express camels to tell that the British army was in full march for Katowlee. These fellows showing an inclination to attack me, and outnumbering my small party of eighty men so much, I thought it right to retire, which I did slowly and deliberately, sending off to Lord Lake a confirmation of the report he had received of Holcar being still at the place. Meantime, the 500 sowars charged me, but in-

though pretending to take part with the British, they allowed the enemy, in disguise, to come into the town, from whence they fired upon our sepoys in the fort, and killed many. They refused, too, to sell the Hindoo sepoys any food, by which they were nearly starved of hunger.

effectually, and having repulsed them I threw
myself into a deserted village to defend myself
until the army should come up. No sooner did
they see Lord Lake's dust than they began to
retire to their camp, on which I followed them for
a côs, charging them twice, and capturing a stand
of colours and about 100 horses. Just as I made
my last charge, Holcar's army was seen about a
côs distant, and the 8th dragoons came up, with
Lord Lake, to my assistance. Holcar's army
having halted, and showing a disposition to attack
us, we also halted to let the rest of the line come
up. But a few rounds from the gallopers sent
them to the right-about, and they dispersed as
they had done at Shamlee. In this service I had
about seven men killed and ten wounded, and my
own horse received a cut on the head. Lord Lake
praised the men very much, and made me a present
of a pair of pistols.

We followed Holcar up to Meerut, but nothing
of consequence occurred. There we left Colonel
Burn's detachment, along with Murray's horse;
and with the reserve alone we followed Holcar,
at the rate of twelve or sixteen côs a day, until we
reached Alleegunge. On the 16th November,
Lord Lake, resolved to overtake Holcar and save

Futtehghur, marched in the evening, leaving my corps, under Colonel Down, with the reserve, to bring up the baggage, and surprised that chief on the morning of the 17th. The execution done that day is well known to the world.* On the morning of the 19th, I arrived with the reserve, and the same evening his lordship sent for me and said he wished much that I would try to discover what route Holcar had taken, and asked, if I thought my corps would undertake the job? I replied, that my corps would obey any orders which his lordship might give; on which he shook me by the hand, and said, " Give me good information, and I shall soon be up with you."

I accordingly returned straight to camp, and leaving all my baggage, galled horses, and gallopers, with my brother (who was dangerously ill), under the care of Major Burrows, who commanded the horse-artillery, I started from Futtehghur at two A.M. on the morning of the 20th, with about 600 sowars, and reached Mynpooree that evening. Holcar, believing that the whole army was upon him, took to flight, while I, sending regular daily information to his lordship, pressed onwards, and saved Mr. Cunningham's

* It has been already taken notice of.

house from being burned, as also that of Captain White, which Holcar was preparing to storm; the Sebundees, who were left under that officer to guard them, being in a great fright; and happy were both officers and civilians to see me that day, declaring, that had I not arrived as I did, they were afraid their own troops would have gone over to Holcar.

On the 21st I started again, and came up with Holcar at Aitah, where I took prisoners about 100 of his sowars. With these I practised a stratagem, which sent Holcar away faster than he bargained for. Telling them that my corps considered them as brethren, I gave them their liberty; but advised them to take care not to fall into the hands of the dragoons, who were but a few hours behind, and bade them give my salaam to Holcar. Thankful for their release, they went and gave my message to Holcar, adding, that they *had seen* Lord Lake and his dragoons. This made him fly faster than ever; but I kept hanging on his rear, marching at the rate of twenty to twenty-five côs a day, until he crossed the Jumna at Mahabun, near Muttra; then I returned to Row-ka-Secundra, near Hattrass, where I halted.

In this hard seven day's work I had no pro-

vision but what the fields afforded, and neither
tents nor bazaar with us. The horses were never
unsaddled, and we rested with the bagdoor (halter,
or leading rein) in our hands all night, having
frequently to change our ground two or three
times during each night, to avoid a surprise from
Holcar. In this pursuit I acquired great plunder
in horses and camels. We lived on the green
jowar that was standing in the fields, which we
prepared by husking it out and putting it into
large pots, adding ghee and meat, and boiling the
whole together. It was then served out in earthen
pots, my share being always brought me by the
men, who showed me great love and attention,
and were willing to act as my private servants,
and tried in every way to please and add to my
comfort; but I felt the want of my dram.

Four days after I came here, Lord Lake arrived,
and the corps paraded to receive him. He came
up and praised them highly, promised that their
services should never be forgotten, and that they
had, by their exertions, secured permanent bread
for their lives. On me also he bestowed high
commendations, giving me a horse with silver
trappings, which had been sent him by some
Rajah, and told me to go back to Alleegurh and

rest for a month, and recruit my corps to 1,700 strong, for that he should soon require my services again. His lordship with the army went to Muttra, and crossing proceeded to Deeg; while I reached Coel in two marches, and commenced recruiting, in which I was very successful; for most of the great powers being now nearly crushed, I was joined by a great number of my old comrades from Perron's service, who had returned to their homes in the Doab.

I had not been here a month out, when an express came from Colonel Boe, who had been repulsed at a small fort near Alleegunge. I hastened to join him; and on my arrival, the garrison attempted to make their escape by night; but they were pursued and cut up almost to a man. This service was performed on a dark night, and several of my men were killed and wounded. We then marched to attack a large mud fort named Imlanee, sixteen côs east of Alleegunge, belonging to a refractory jemadar, named Nahur Allee. We besieged it for a month, and were twice beaten back in attempts to storm it. But at length, two mines being carried under the glacis, the garrison tried to make their escape : they were pursued by my

brother, who killed 300 of them; the rest, with
Nahur Allee, succeeded in making good their
flight. My brother had his horse killed under
him.

On the 23rd December, Lord Lake stormed
and took Deeg, and then marched to invest
Bhurtpore. Having returned to the army, I
was ordered by Major Worsely to escort a large
convoy of a lakh of bullocks loaded with atta
and wheat from Anoopsheher. Thither I went,
and receiving charge of the Brinjarrahs passed
within two côs of Kamoona, a place held in great
dread in the Doab. Keeping 400 of my horse
in a body, I dispersed the rest among the bullocks, when, all of a sudden, out darted Doondiah
Khan with 600 sowârs. I attacked him with my
400, and chased him back to the ditch of his fort,
with the loss of 200 of his men killed; and delivered over the convoy safe at Muttra, which
gained me many commendations from his Excellency, as well as Major Worsely.

I had returned to Alleeghur, when Colonel
Gruiber, with his battalion, was attacked by the
same Doondiah Khan, and obliged to fall back on
Anoopsheher, where he was joined by some provincial battalions, under command of Captain

Cruttenden. I again received orders from Major Worsely to join Colonel Gruiber, and did accordingly join him within two côs of Kamoona. Proceeding thence to Alleeghur, I was ordered to receive and escort 30,000 Brinjarrahs loaded with atta to the grand army, which convoy I delivered just after the first storm of Bhurtpore had failed. I met with no molestation from Muttra till within a côs of Bhurtpore, when Bappojee Sindeah was sent out to attack me. He came up with 1,000 horse; but Lord Lake having sent out a detachment to my aid, Bappoo, on seeing them, retreated.

Next morning, I marched for Muttra, and from thence again proceeded to Coel to join Colonel Gruiber, who was ordered to attack Kamoona. I came up with him at Chuttooree, a village about a côs from Kamoona, and marched next morning with the detachment to the bank of the Kalee Muddee, on the east of Kamoona, where we encamped. We besieged the place for a month, during which time my corps was hard worked, and many acts of gallantry were performed by the men in presence of the whole detachment. My brother himself had two horses killed under him.

CHAPTER XIII.

Ameer Khan—His birth and early history—Combines forces
with Holcar—Terms of agreement—His army and military
system—Character—Crosses the Jumna on a predatory
expedition — General Smith sent in pursuit — Siege of
Kamoona raised—Mr. Leicester and the Europeans at
Bareilly surrounded by Ameer Khan—Relieved by Skin-
ner's arrival—Pursuit of the Meer—Skinner visits his
camp in disguise—Attack on his army near Ufzoolghur—
Retires with loss towards Mooradabad — The younger
Skinner surrounded—His gallant defence—Relieved by a
stratagem of his brother's—Captain Murray attacked by
Meer Khan—Driven off by Colonel Burn—He retreats
across the Jumna — Failure at Bhurtpore — Kamoona
capitulates—Services of Skinner's corps—Acknowledged
by Lord Lake—Expedition against the Sikhs—Holcar
appears in the Punjaub—Pursued by Lord Lake— Skinner
volunteers to cross the Sutlej—The army crosses—He is
sent in advance to track Holcar—Reaches the Beyah, or
Hyphasis—Negotiations with Holcar—Review of troops—
Effect on the Sikhs—Return to Kurnaul—Partial reduc-
tion of Skinner's corps — The army broken up.

THE next portion of the memoir relates in great
part to the well-known "foray" of the celebrated

freebooter, Ameer Khan, into Rohilcund, his native place, having crossed the whole Doab and its two great streams, at the head of his followers, in the usual Pindarree fashion, with nothing but his horse and his arms. And it is now time to give some account of the origin and rise of this remarkable predatory chief.

Mahomed Ameer Khan was the son of Illyat Khan, a Patan of the Tereen tribe, originally from Affghanistan; and who lived at a village near Sumbhul in the Zillah of Mooradabad, named Seraee-Tereen—the abode of the Tereens. When about twenty years of age he left his home for the Dekhan, then the great theatre for soldiers of fortune, with ten followers; and entered into several services, in which he so far prospered as to increase his followers to six horsemen and sixty foot. But his first engagement of consequence was with Jeysing Keechee of Ragooghur, who, with his relative, Dourjun Lal, had been ousted from their territories by Sindea, and who now maintained themselves by pillaging the same lands they had once possessed. But a quarrel with a favourite of the latter chief, terminating in a squabble in which Ameer Khan was severely wounded, led to his quitting that service, in which

he had much distinguished himself, and been presented by the Rajah with a palankin and the
command of 500 men. He then entered into that
of Balaram, a predatory leader of Sindea's, at that
time subsisting in Bhopal on pillage, and afterwards called in to aid one of the parties who were
struggling for power in that state. By him he
was promoted to the charge of 1,500 horse and
of the strong fortress of Futtehghur, the citadel of
Bhopal.

The course of intrigue soon occasioned the departure of the Mahrattas from Bhopal; but Ameer
Khan retained possession of Futtighur, and only
gave it up to one of the disputing parties on being
taken into the service. But his own intriguing
spirit rendered him too dangerous a character to
be long retained. After six months he left it, or
was dismissed, and it was at this period that the
attention of Jesswunt Rao Holcar, who was then
just rising into something of importance, became
directed to the Patan leader. The first meeting
between these celebrated freebooters took place
at Ranagunge, near Shujahalpore, and they soon
came to terms. Ameer Khan entered into engagements never to desert the fortunes of Jesswunt Rao; and received a written promise from

that chief that all future plunder or conquest should be shared equally between them. With men of such characters and equally desperate fortunes, it is probable that an agreement, thus entered into from mutual convenience, would scarcely have been held binding any longer than the interests of either party might seem to dictate; and yet certainly Ameer Khan did continue his fidelity to Holcar long after the latter had attained to sovereign power—a fact to be accounted for probably from the strong influence of Holcar's more energetic character, and the tact which he always exhibited in distinguishing the Patan from his other leaders, even after the relations of prince and dependant were clearly established between them.* Ameer Khan remained sole commander of his own army, and entertained or dismissed whom he would. "But," says Sir John Malcolm,† "his condition was little to be envied. His followers, who were always more numerous than he had the means of paying, were in a state of constant mutiny; and for more than half of every year, their chief was

---

* He always called the Meer "brother," and affected to regard him as of equal rank with himself.

† "Central India," vol. i. p. 327-28

under restraint. The consequence was, that his
conduct was always more regulated by the
clamours of this turbulent rabble, and the necessity of providing for their support, than by any
regular system of policy.   The excesses of Ameer
Khan's Patans at Saugur have been noticed; but
these were far surpassed at Poonah, where he was
seized by a party of them, and not only beat and
bruised, but almost strangled with his own turban,
which they fastened round his neck.   Though
Jesswunt Rao repressed and punished this act of
violence, he, too, on many occasions was compelled to soothe and humour the turbulent spirits
of the freebooters. . . . . It was the constant object of Jesswunt Rao to employ them at
a distance, and he appears to have considered
them more as a body of plunderers, whose general
movements he could direct through his connection
with their leader, than as an integral portion of
his army, whose services he could at all times
command.   They, on the other hand, were sensible of the advantages they derived from acting
in the name of one of the recognised Indian
governments; and the main influence by which
Ameer Khan retained his precarious rank as
their chief, was his forming the link that at-

tached this band of depredators to the house of
Holcar."

Meer Khan's expedition into Rohilcund appears to have partly originated in the mutual
disputes and taunts of the confederates, in consequence of their ill-success in their war with the
English ; and the Meer, perhaps, imagined that
he should not only succeed better in his open
system of depredation, but increase his power and
forces in his own country, which was filled with
desperate characters.   Born a Patan, he naturally
leant to prefer his countrymen, although, latterly,
the great preponderance of them in his army may
have tended not only to curb his own authority,
but to perpetuate the mischief they occasioned.
It is obvious that he was deficient in that first
qualification in a captain of banditti, the power to
overawe and command his men.   He was, in fact,
not so much their chief as their slave—only tolerated as the head to contrive their expeditions,
the pilot to lead them to their prey.   He was
even regarded as deficient in personal courage,
and more of a blusterer than a doer.   The marking features of his character appear to have been,
a strong turn for intrigue, indefatigable cunning,
insatiable avarice, and remorseless, unscrupulous

cruelty. He wanted the reckless boldness in
crime, the audacious defiance of all principle,
exhibited by Holcar, and he was far from being
possessed of that prince's undaunted courage. He
had more of the tiger than the lion—perhaps, more
of the serpent than of either; and while the sweep-
ing devastation of the Mahratta prince seems to
have been regarded as an act of destiny,—a visi-
tation of Providence, apart from its author,—the
atrocities of the Patan are held in detestation
over all Hindostan, as spontaneous works of a
cruel and evil-hearted ruffian.

Nor were the manners of the Meer more attractive than his character. He is represented, by
those who have seen and known him, as clownish
and rude in appearance and address; mean in person; of dark Hindoo-like complexion; poorly and
dirtily dressed, and his language low and coarse.
The result of his visit to his country seems in no
respect to have answered his expectations. He
came over the Ganges with 30,000 followers, and a
name which, as a leader, carried terror at least with
it, and might have been attractive to soldiers of
fortune like himself. He re-crossed that river
and the Doab, baffled, beaten, disgraced, his
troops reduced to a third of their number, and

his name sunk into a word of derision and contempt.

At this juncture, says Skinner, and on the 3rd of February, Ameer Khan crossed the Jumna; on which Major Worsely sent an express to Colonel Grüber, who, on receiving it, raised the siege of Kamoona, and retired under Alleeghur. On the the 9th, General Smith, with three regiments of dragoons, three of native cavalry, and a detachment of horse-artillery, sent by Lord Lake, came to our assistance. About twelve at night we marched, and, my corps being sent in advance, we reached Meer Khan's encampment before Kamoona at daybreak, and found he had taken himself off two hours before our arrival.

We came up, however, with an alleegole* of about 300 Rohillas, belonging to Doondiah Khan, whom we attacked and cut up, following them to the brink of the ditch. About seven in the morning General Smith came up, and gave my men high commendation for their conduct.

Next morning, while marching a couple of côs

* Alleegoles were a sort of chosen light infantry of the Rohilla Patans: sometimes the term appears to be applied to other troops, supposed to be used generally for desperate service.

in two lines, the cavalry being on our right, Colonel Grüber was insulted by a small fort, called Annoona, belonging to Doondiah Khan, which he stormed and took, with the loss of one European officer killed, and twenty sepoys killed and wounded. On the 13th, the Colonel's detachment was ordered to proceed by Anopsheher, while the cavalry pushed on after Ameer Khan, who crossed the Ganges at Ahmednaghur on the 15th, and went straight for Mooradabad. We followed on his track, and on the 17th reached Amronah.

At noon the same day, I was sent off with 1,000 horse, to relieve Mr. Leicester,* who, with all the party at Bareilly, was surrounded in the gaol of that place. General Smith himself followed us. I reached the place a little before dawn of the 18th, and found that Meer Khan had just left it. We followed him as far as the Ramgunga, and, overtaking his rear-guard, cut up 300 of his sowars; after which we returned to Mr. Leicester's house. An hour after sunrise General Smith, with the cavalry, reached the place.

Our arrival at the time we did was the most

* Chief of the civil service at Bareilly.

fortunate thing possible, for the sebundees* who were on duty would have given up the Europeans and treasure; and it is impossible to describe the joy with which we were hailed by the whole party, which had been surrounded by the Meer in this fortified place. Next morning we marched in pursuit; but Meer Khan had led us such a dance, that, for several days, we were all in the dark as to whither he had gone, and we kept marching backwards and forwards until we reached Shereghurrie, when I fell in with, and made prisoners of, some Pindarrees, from whom I made out the proper direction. As soon as this was done, I went secretly to General Smith, and volunteered to go disguised into the Meer's camp, and learn what he was about. To this, after a good deal of hesitation, General Smith agreed; and, accordingly, putting on a native's dress, I took ten of my most confidential sowars, and, giving out to my corps that I was going upon urgent business to Mooradabad, I went straight to Sherekote, where I met with Meer Khan's foragers, and with them went into their camp.

My ten sowars had brethren in Shahmut Khan's

* Hired irregular troops.

gole, and with it we remained all night. Early
in the morning Meer Khan, who was pitched on
the banks of the Ramgunga river, near Ufzulghur, wanted to march; but the Mahratta Pindarrees, who had all been insulted the day before
by the Patans, insisted on the Meer giving up
the offenders. This was refused by the Patans,
upon which both parties drew up to fight. All
this information was sent off by me to General
Smith, by hircarrahs; and when I saw that the
fellows were not likely to settle their disputes
that day, I thought it would be an excellent
thing if I could bring the troops upon them. A
foraging party belonging to Shahmut Khan, being
just about to go out, I took the opportunity of
quitting camp with it, especially as Meer Khan
by this time had settled the dispute, and was proposing to march next morning.

I had not gone two côs, when I met one of
my own spies, who informed me that the army
was just going to encamp at Sherekote. On this
I galloped off, and met General Smith, to whom
I gave all this information, and begged that the
troops might push on, as he might never again
meet with so good an opportunity. The General
thanked me for my exertions, and pushed on to

Sherekote, where he left the baggage under protection of the 3rd regiment of Native Cavalry,
400 sowars, and about 700 nujeebs of mine. In
the mean time I changed my horse and dress, and
then showed them the road.

We came up with the enemy about two P. M.;
but Meer Khan had got intelligence of our approach, and, having sent his baggage on to Ufzulghur, was standing his ground with all his horse,
and a small body of 300 alleegoles, which he had
entertained at Rampore. As our line came up, there
was a nullah just in our front, the ford of which I
was directed to point out to the horse-artillery.
I accordingly accompanied Captain Stark on this
service, showing him the ford, where the troops
crossed and formed in two lines, keeping the river
on our right flank.

Meer Khan now broke up into three goles; one,
being commanded by himself, advanced to our left;
one, commanded by his brother* Shahmut Khan,
took its way to our right; while the third and
smaller one, with the unfortunate 300 alleegoles,
remained in our front. These fellows opened their

---

* The wording in the original is of doubtful meaning;
but, at all events, there is reason for believing that Shahmut
Khan was not a brother of the Meer's.

matchlocks upon us; but a few rounds from the horse-artillery forced them to advance to the shelter of a hollow that was in our front. The 27th Dragoons dashed forward to cut them up; but the fellows, who must have been mad, rushed sword in hand, with their flags, upon the dragoons, penetrated their ranks, and caused some confusion in the regiment. Major Dean, however, charged them with a squadron of the 8th, and cut them to pieces.

Shahmut Khan then charged the right; but was repulsed with great loss by the gallopers and the 29th Dragoons. Meer Khan in person charged my corps on the left with a large gole. My men behaved most gallantly, giving fire with their matchlocks at the word of command; and then drawing swords, they charged and repulsed them with great slaughter; we killed two of their sirdars, took one prisoner, with ten stand of colours, among which were two golden ones, carried by ackas, and 200 horses. My brother Robert's conduct this day surpassed all I had ever seen him perform before. One of my gallopers on the left having got rather far away from the corps, and unlimbered about 100 yards from my flank, an *acka** of Meer Khan's, with about forty

* Probably from the Turkish word *Aga*—leader, master.

sowars, charged and took it. My brother (Lieut. Skinner) observing this, immediately charged them with twenty choice men, retook the galloper, and cut down the acka with his own hand.

The Meer now retired out of cannon reach, and formed into one mass before us; but it being now four P.M., General Smith thought it proper to retreat to his baggage. Meer Khan, on the other hand, had been so sickened with the gallopers that he would venture on nothing; but retreated to Ufzulghur. He certainly gave us fine opportunities for a charge this day; but it was thought that their goles were too large, and were only kept off by our gallopers. My loss was five men killed and thirty wounded; the General gave great praise to our corps, and reported our exertions to Lord Lake, who gave orders to the resident at Dehlee to present me with a fine Persian sword.

We marched in pursuit of Ameer Khan towards Mooradabad, which direction he had taken from Ufzulghur; and arriving at six in the evening, we deposited there all our sick and wounded. My brother was ordered with 500 sowars to Anopsheher, while we marched towards Chaundousee. On arriving there we found that Meer

Khan had been beforehand with us, having burned
the cantonments, and laid the town under contribution; after which he took his way in the direction of Bareilly.   On the 8th, we made a forced
march, and took up our position on the bank of
the Ramgunga, where the river was fordable, in
order to prevent his crossing; and scarcely had
we pitched, when the dreadful intelligence was
brought me that my brother was surrounded by
Ameer Khan in a ruinous serai in Sumbul, into
which he had thrown himself on hearing of the
Meer's approach.

From the account given me by the messenger,
it appeared that when the party were thus hem-
med in, Ameer Khan had written to the rissaldars,
desiring them to give my brother up, and that he
would give each of them three months' pay as a
reward.   This they refused contemptuously, upon
which the Meer advanced with 10,000 men dismounted, towards the serai, and sent the same message again, to which he received the same reply.

My brother now, in order to test the men's
fidelity, addressed them and told them, that if, by
giving up his single life, they could save 500, he
was quite willing to give himself up, and go as a
prisoner to Ameer Khan.   To this they replied,

that when they were all destroyed he might go,
but not as long as they lived. That they did not
mind numbers—hundreds, they said, were daily
destroyed at Bhurtpore; they also were soldiers
hired to die, therefore let them die like soldiers.

My brother then wrote to Ameer Khan, declaring that he had always believed him to be a
brave soldier, but that his conduct this day, in
attempting to seduce and delude the soldiers
under his command, whose courage and fidelity
he should soon have experience of, had proved
him to be a coward, that he despised him and
dared him to come on. As soon as the messenger
was despatched, and he saw the Meer's people
moving, he told his men to kneel down and offer
their last prayers to God to grant them courage,
and to die like brave men. The storm now took
place on all sides, but it was nobly repulsed by
my men. Many of the enemy got up upon the
walls, and were cut down from them in trying to
get over. Three times did they assault, and each
time they were repulsed with great slaughter.
When it got dark the spy left my brother,
having spent all his ammunition except a few
rounds. During the night, he took the shoes
from off his horse's feet, and cut them into slugs,

of which he distributed five to each man, which, with five bullets remaining to each, was all he had to repel the multitude around him. But the men remained stanch and firm to him, and he besought me to come to his aid without delay.

I went instantly to General Smith, crying and entreating him to march, or to allow me to go to my brother's assistance, that I would cut my way through Meer Khan's troops, and get into the serai, which was only twenty côs off, in time to save him. But, as it was three P. M. before the letter reached me, General Smith declared that it was useless; that the Meer must either have destroyed the party or gone off from the place, as Colonel Burn was in that quarter. As for him, he could not, he said, leave the ford. This hope failing me, I was utterly at a loss how to act, when the following stratagem occurred to me, and I instantly put it in practice. I wrote a letter to my brother, saying I had just received his, and had shewn it to the General, who was about to march with his whole force in an hour or two; in the mean time, he must keep the Meer in play by proposing terms of surrender. One of my hircarrahs, who had been brought up in my family, volunteered to have this delivered to Meer Khan, and ten of my sowars, who were equally confidential, took in hand to play him a trick in aid of the plan. To the hircarrah I promised 800 rupees, and a thousand to the sowars. They all left me at four P. M., and General Smith himself agreed to march at midnight.

The hircarrah and sowars got within a còs of Meer Khan's position about dawn of day, and got information that my brother was still safe, and had repulsed another storm on the last evening. Being a clever fellow, he came to the following arrangement with the sowars, namely, that just at daybreak they should set fire to several stacks of *khurbee* (corn-straw) that were in the fields, while he should contrive to be taken by the piquets, and of course be brought before the Meer. This he easily made out, and being taken to Meer Khan, he confessed at once that he had been sent by me, who was very much attached to my brother. That he had understood the sahib had been taken prisoner, and was in his camp, so he had come to fulfil the service he engaged to perform as a faithful servant. That the Meer might do with him what he pleased, only let him be permitted to see his master.

Meer Khan had the letter read, and then asked

the hircarrah when the army would move. He
replied that the orders issued were, that they
should move at midnight. Whilst this was going
on, the sowars had put fire to the stacks, and then
they chased in a few camp followers, who had
gone out upon business of their own. In a moment the cry arose that the English had arrived,
upon which Meer Khan immediately saddled and
mounted, ordered the hircarrah to receive a few
stripes, and in a few hours not one of them was to
be seen. The hircarrah and the sowars then went
to my brother, who welcomed them very warmly.

We had marched about nine côs, when information reached us of my brother's safety and
Ameer Khan's flight, and next morning my
brother joined me at Circey, and was cordially
welcomed for his gallant conduct, not only by me,
but by the whole army. The whole affair met
with high praise from General Smith, and was
reported to his Excellency, Lord Lake, who
wrote a Persian letter to the men, applauding
them for their conduct. My brother's loss in this
business was ten killed and about fifty wounded.
That of Meer Khan was about a thousand in
both. The hircarrah and sowars were very handsomely rewarded, and we all resumed our march

after Ameer Khan, who had retired in the direction of Amrowah.

By this time, having lost his name in the country, and being deserted by many of his soldiers, every walled village opposed him, and he now pushed on towards the ford. On his way he attacked Captain Murray, who threw himself into a walled village, and repulsed the attack with a loss to his assailants of several hundred men. Colonel Burn soon arrived to the assistance of Murray, who succeeded in capturing the Meer's bazaar. On the 13th Meer Khan crossed with only about 10,000 men out of the 30,000 which he had brought with him from Bhurtpore.

Our news from that place, however, was very disheartening, and threw a damp over the whole detachment. We recrossed the Ganges at the same ghaut where we passed it a month before in our chase after the Meer. We marched at the rate of fifteen or twenty miles a day, and on the 18th came before Kamoona, the chief of which was now much humbled, and entreated General Smith to procure his forgiveness from his Excellency. This the General did obtain for this villain, who afterwards proved to be a traitor, and the cause of many valuable lives being lost. On the 19th

we arrived before Alleeghur, where we learned
that Ameer Khan had recrossed the Jumna. I
accompanied General Smith to Hanseagunge,
opposite to Muttra, from whence I was ordered
back to Coel. I reached that place on the 27th,
terminating a course of the severest service
that any corps had ever gone through. In the
chase after Holcar the army had gone 500 miles,
in that after Meer Khan 700 miles, and mine was
the only Hindostanee corps during all that time
that continued throughout the chase. It performed all the duties of the camp, and, to the best
of my belief, was never less than eighteen hours
out of the twenty-four on horseback. The hard-
ships endured by my men, who were constantly
out, were well known to the commander and
officers of the two detachments. On the smallest
calculation, they underwent in these two chases
full twice the labour and hardship endured by the
regulars, and often in the chase after Meer Khan,
when my men had the rear-guard, have they
picked up the European dragoons who were
knocked up on the march, and dismounting, put
them on their own horses, and led them thus to
camp, conduct which made them beloved by the
dragoons: and notwithstanding this hard duty,

they never murmured, nor were once accused of
disobeying any order whatsoever; and never did
they turn their backs before the enemy, though
frequently opposed to far superior numbers.   His
Excellency's kindness towards the corps was great,
and whenever service was to be performed, I was
sure of being sent for, which was a matter of the
greatest consolation and satisfaction to me, and
gave me spirits to undergo my labour cheerfully,
knowing that if anything were done, it would not
fail of being acknowledged by his lordship.   In
these two campaigns, I had the satisfaction of
receiving from his Excellency two swords and a
pair of pistols, a circumstance which was regarded
as a mark of great favour and approbation.

At Alleeghur I remained about fifteen days,
when my brother, with 700 sowars, was ordered
to join Colonel Richardson on an expedition
against Toorkapoorah, a fort belonging to Naher
Allee of Emlanee.   I at the same time was sent
with the remainder of my corps, to escort 30,000
Brinjarrahs to the army at Bhurtpore.   I delivered my charge safe, and returned to Alleeghur, when I received orders to join the detachment of Colonel Burn, near Saharunpore, which
was at this time again attacked by all the Sikhs.

I marched to Dehlee, where General Ochterlony
reviewed the corps, on whom he bestowed great
praise, and presented me with a sword taken from
his own waist, in Lord Lake's name, and in front
of the corps. I then pursued my march to join
Colonel Burn; but before I could join them,
which I did at Kurnaul, he had succeeded in driving the Sikhs across the Jumna; and in a short
time afterwards, the whole of the Sikh Rajahs
came to terms. Lord Lake had also compelled the
Bhurtpore man to the same course, and having completed treaties with Sindea and several Rajahs, he
broke up his camp and retired to cantonments at
Muttra, Agra, and Futtehpore Seekree, for the
rains. Col. Burn returned to Paneeput, where we
built temporary cantonments, and Holcar, having
no home to go to, retreated with the sad remains
of his troops to Jhoudpore. Meer Khan, having
now only about 10,000 men left, followed his
fortunes.

On the 1st October 1805, however, Holcar,
who had contrived to recruit his troops in Raj-
pootanah, and to collect some artillery, marched
towards the Punjab, in hopes of receiving assistance from the Sikhs, who, it was said, particularly
Runjeet Singh, had actually made some promise

to that effect. Together with Ameer Khan's force, he could now muster about 30,000 horse, 10,000 infantry, and about forty pieces of cannon, and with this force he marched through the Hurrianah country. When he arrived at a point on our west, we moved out from Paneeput to give him a check, but were too late; he had passed us, so we marched after him, and on the 29th November at Rawseana, we were joined by his Excellency Lord Lake. On the 2nd December we reached Loodianah; but Holcar had already crossed the Sutlej, and was only sixteen côs from us at a place called Jullunder.

Certain political considerations prevented Lord Lake from crossing; but when he found that Holcar would not move, he on the evening of the 3rd, at dinner, observed that he wished some one would try the ford with a troop and galloper. Colonel Worsely told me that the hint was intended for me, on which I immediately rose and said,—" If your lordship will give me leave, I will try the ford to-morrow morning." He replied,—" Be there about dawn, with two rissalahs of your yellow boys and a galloper, and I will also be with you." I bowed and sat down again. Next morning, with two choice rissalahs and a galloper, I was ready at the ghaut, where his lordship, with the whole of his staff and a number of officers from the camp, soon arrived. Colonel Malcolm, who was one of the political agents, dismounted along with his Excellency, and argued the point of my crossing; but I heard his lordship reply that he took the responsibility upon himself. He then mounted, and coming up to me, said,—"Well, are you ready?" "Yes, my lord," replied I. "Well then, dash forward," said he. Upon this I made my salaam, and giving three cheers, dashed on.

Our horses had to swim for about twenty yards, after which they got footing. There was an island in the middle of the river, to which I bent my course. On reaching this, we discovered it to be a quicksand, in which my galloper stuck fast. I immediately dismounted, and directed my brother, with the two rissalahs, to cross, and then dismounting one of them, to bring the men back to relieve the galloper which had now sunk up to the wheels. In less than an hour the rissalah returned, took out the horses, and dragged the gun across; and just as we landed, I took off my hat, and giving three hurrahs, in which Colonel Malcolm and all Lord Lake's staff joined, proclaimed that the first British gun had crossed the Sutlej.

A few Sikhs made their appearance, and the rissalah was ordered to drive them off, and no sooner had it mounted than away they run. We returned and sounded the ford, putting up posts to shew the road; and the work terminated by Lord Lake making a present of 5,000 rupees to the two rissalahs for their activity and willingness.

On the 5th, next morning, a battalion of sepoys was ordered across to secure the ford. Still Holcar kept his ground; but when, on the morning of the 6th, the whole army crossed, and on the 7th commenced our march towards the Beyah, Holcar moved on, and crossed that river. Next day, the 8th, I was sent on with 400 sowars to find out if he had actually crossed; and, after a march of about thirty miles, succeeded in getting a glance at his army which had crossed that morning. Just as I reached the left bank, his rear-guard, who were on the opposite one, fired a few shots at us from an eighteen-pounder. They had been waiting for about 1,000 Brinjarrah bullocks which had gone out for supplies; but falling in with them on my return to camp, I took them prisoners, and about midnight brought them all in with me. I had this day marched with the army twenty miles, ten more to the river bank, and ten more back to camp—in all, forty miles.

Next morning, the 9th December, I went on with the army to a point opposite to Bojepore ghaut. From this place the pillar of *Secunder** was distant ten côs to the west, and my horse was the first of the British camp to taste the water of the HYPHASIS.

On the 19th, Holcar's vakeels, accompanied by those of Runjeet Sing, came into camp, for such was the firmness and decision of his Excellency, that the whole business was brought to a peaceful termination. The bold arrogance of the Sikhs, and the vapouring declarations of Holcar, and his determination of making his saddle his house† until he had accomplished his purposes, were all cowed and humbled by the gallantry of a force not exceeding 1,000 British troops, and to the astonishment of the whole Indian world.

In order to give them an idea of what these troops were, his Excellency gave a review of the

---

* Alexander the Great.

† Holcar had more than once, in correspondence as well as by word of mouth, declared, in Mahratta phrase, that his home and house was the back of his horse, and wherever that horse's head pointed became his country.

force to Futteh Sing Alwah, Runjeet's second in command; indeed, some asserted that Runjeet himself was present in disguise. They were amazed at the performances of the Europeans and horse artillery, and especially when the horse artillery dashed through intervals of cavalry after a charge, and fired within fifty yards of the spot where these great folks were standing. It was all astonishment, and a general cry burst from the Sikhs of "Wah Gooroo, Wah Gooroo!" "Jadoo kurdeah!" " Oh saints, oh saints, it is all witchcraft!"*

On the 9th of January 1806, we left these plains where the great Alexander of old astonished the famous Rajah Phoor, and retraced our steps to Kurnaul. On the 20th February, I was left with my corps at that place along with Colonel Burn, who was directed to remain there. Lord Lake did not come up till the 25th, but he halted here upwards of two months, discharging the irregular troops with pensions and jaghires. My corps, which had amounted to 1,700, was

* Major Thorn confirms this effect of the sight of our military manoeuvres on the Sikhs, and adds, that they were heard whispering to one another, " Thank God, we did not go to war with the English."

reduced to 1,200, the remaining 500 being discharged and all the officers pensioned; and it was the only irregular cavalry retained and made permanent, as a reward for their fidelity and exertions. Having thus arranged matters, and Holcar having passed Dehlee on his return, his lordship broke up the army and marched with the Europeans to Cawnpore.

CHAPTER VI.

The Marquis Cornwallis relieves Lord Wellesley—Change of policy—Lord Cornwallis dies—Is succeeded by Sir George Barlow—Economy and reduction—Reduction of Skinner's corps—Disappointments—Negotiations for a provision for the Skinners—Further disappointments—Skinner patronized by Mr. Seton—Raises a corps for the settlement of Hurriana —Letters from friends—From the Marquis of Hastings—Rise of the Pindarrees—Their chiefs—And respective strength—Their modes of plundering—Account of a luhbur or foray—Scheme of the Mahratta and Pindarree war—Battles of Khirkee, Seetabuldee, and Mehidpore—Affair of Corrygaon—Death of Holcar—Intrigues in his family—Arrangements with Sindea—Destruction of the Pindarrees—Fate of Cheetoo—Of Kurreem Khan—Termination and consequences of the war.

BUT events had for some time been in progress, which were destined sadly to damp the satisfaction which Skinner had felt at the termination of the campaign, in finding so large a portion of his corps retained permanently on the strength of the service. A change of policy at home led to a change of government in India. The Marquis of Cornwallis was sent out to relieve Lord Wellesley; and his lordship had no sooner arrived in India, than he turned his attention to establishing peace, on any terms, with all the native powers; and to the reduction of expense in every branch of the service. These measures involved a wide departure from the bold and successful policy of his predecessor, and serious sacrifices of principles hitherto adhered to, with the extensive alterations in the military establishment of the company; and though, while Holcar was still in arms, and Sindea threatening, immediate reduction was impossible, the first moment of success was seized with avidity for bringing into play the purposed economical reforms.

On the 5th of October, Lord Cornwallis, worn out with age and illness, expired at Ghazeepore, and was succeeded by Sir George Barlow, the senior member of council, who adopted to the full all the cautious and conciliatory principles of his predecessor. His views were entirely adverse to defensive alliances and subsidiary forces, and to all sorts of interference with the states west of the Jumna. With them, therefore, former treaties were abandoned,* and in the same spirit, an arrangement was entered into with Sindea, on very favourable terms for the latter. The same indulgence was also extended to Holcar, who, from his treacherous hostility, still less merited such leniency.

In all these measures his Excellency differed very widely from the opinions entertained by the Commander-in-Chief, Lord Lake, who failed not to remonstrate strongly against their impolicy and evil tendency. Nor did events long fail of proving the correctness of his views, and how ill a timid or vacillating policy was suited for dealing with the native powers of India. The rapid growth of predatory bands, and general anarchy and confusion in Central India, indicated the justice of his lordship's calculation and prophetic fears.

Meantime, peace and economy being the order of the day, curtailment of expenditure and reduction of the military followed of course, and among the rest, Skinner's remaining corps of 1,200 horse, though guaranteed as permanent by Lord Lake,

* The Rajah of Jeypore, in particular, was desirous of British protection; but he, as well as the rest of the Rajepoot states, was refused.

was ordered to be paid off. This very unpleasant order was communicated to poor Skinner by his lordship himself, in a manner which shows the high regard he felt for that officer, and his sense of the injustice of which he was compelled to be the instrument towards him. The general order for discharging the corps is dated the 11th April 1806, and their pay is thereby ordered to be made good only to the 20th. It terminates by the following testimony to their good and faithful service :—

"On this occasion, the Commander-in-Chief is pleased to record the high sense which he entertains of the valuable services rendered by Captain Skinner, and the corps under his command during the war; and his lordship will not fail to report to Government the zealous and successful manner in which Captain Skinner has invariably discharged the duties of his important station.

"As a further remark of his lordship's estimation of the fidelity and good conduct of the corps, he authorizes a gratuity equal to a month's pay each, to be given to all the native officers and men now ordered to be discharged.

(Signed)   "T. WORSELY,

"Deputy Adjutant-General."

My mind, says Skinner, had been made quite easy by the late arrangements, when suddenly an express arrived from Lord Lake, desiring that I should immediately repair to head-quarters. I immediately overtook him at Secundra, where he was sitting at breakfast, and was very kindly received. After breakfast, his lordship retired to his tent, whither I was soon sent for, and found Colonels Malcolm and Worsley with him. With tears in his eyes he gave me the despatch from Sir George Barlow, which contained the order to discharge my corps. I read it, but said nothing, when his lordship catching me by the hand, said, " Skinner, I regret this much—what can I do for you?" " My lord," I replied, " if you are satisfied with my conduct, I am repaid for all my exertions. The character you have already given me will procure me bread; and some just man may here-after come to the head of affairs, who, from your recommendation, may again take me by the hand." " Well," said he, " but how can I satisfy you now?" I replied that I should be contented with a small jagheer, as I did not mean again to serve as a soldier, unless obliged to do so. He asked how much would satisfy me and my brother, to which I replied, that I desired to leave it all to his lordship. He then consulted a while aside with Colonel Malcolm, and turning to me, asked if 20,000 rupees a year would satisfy both of us? I immediately thanked him, and said he was making princes of us. He laughed, and then appointed jagheers of 5,000 rupees a year a piece to four of my rissaldars, pensioned all the officers as low as duffehdars,* gave three months' pay as gratuity to the rest of the corps, and placed all the wounded men upon the Hauper establishment. I then took my leave, with a letter to the collector of Coel, for my jaghire; and returning, brought the corps to Dehlee, where the painful task awaited me of tearing myself from the men who had gained me such laurels in the British service. All those who had deserted that service at first, and then came over to it, received rewards. Those only who had proved themselves all along faithful servants were discharged from it.

Poor Skinner, however, had not, as he says, learned the worst of his hard fate; no sooner had he parted from his brave comrades, and gone to Coel to take possession of his jagheer, than he received a letter from Colonel Malcolm, informing him, that *being a British subject*, Sir George Bar-

* Commanders of ten.

low could not permit him to hold land, so that he found himself, after all his zealous services, and after many sincerely meant promises, thrown adrift without provision or reward. The orders of the Governor-General were not of course, to be disputed; but his steady friend, Lord Lake, again interfered, and he received another letter from Colonel Malcolm in the following terms :—

" MY DEAR SKINNER, — Lord Lake has recommended you in the strongest terms to government, and I have no doubt but you will be placed upon the footing of Lieutenant-Colonel in the Mahratta service, whatever that may be. With respect to your wishes for land, Lord Lake will authorize me to speak upon the subject when I go to Calcutta, and you may be satisfied of my hearty endeavours to accomplish the object you desire, and that I shall rejoice if I am at all instrumental in promoting the success of a person for whose character I entertain the sincerest respect, and of the validity of whose claim upon the public service, I have had the best opportunities of forming a correct judgment.

(Signed) " JNO. MALCOLM."
" Cawnpore, 7th June, 1806."

It appears that subsequently Skinner himself,

H 2

doubtless acting by the advice of his friends, wrote to the Governor-General on the same subject, and the result of the negociation was a communication from Mr. Edmonstone, secretary to Government, to Captain Skinner, intimating that the Governor-General in Council, with reference to the claims of those officers who had quitted the Mahratta service in conformity with the Governor-General's proclamation of August 1803, had authorized his drawing the allowances to which he had been previously entitled up to the 1st of October; and further, that considering the sacrifice of prospects in the Mahratta service, and the circumstances under which it was made, he is satisfied that the grant of a pension for life, equal to the amount of retiring allowances of officers of equal rank in the Company's service, would constitute an adequate remuneration for officers in that position. But, with reference to the special services rendered by the applicant himself, since quitting the Mahratta service, and the sense which "Government entertains of your general merits and character," the Governor-General had been induced to assign to him as remuneration, the amount of the nett full pay of the rank of colonel in the Honourable Company's service; and accordingly, Captain Skinner is authorized to draw during his life, as pension, 300 Sonaut rupees per month, with permission to reside in any part of the Company's territories, or to proceed to Europe, at his option.

This, said Skinner, was all that Lord Lake could obtain for me; *my four rissaldars got each of them more;* but I resolved in my own mind to remain quiet, and see what further misfortunes there might be for me to bear. In the mean time, I received from his Excellency a letter, telling me that what he had obtained now was for the present only; but that as soon as he should reach home, he would get the Court of Directors to confirm me in my jagheer, and also to replace my 1,200 men on permanent service, in spite of Sir George Barlow. I wrote in return a letter, expressive of my thanks, and assured his lordship, that I had every confidence in his desire to serve me; but that fate, I feared, was against me. However, happen what might, I should always most gratefully acknowledge his lordship's kindness and favour.

I now sat myself down in Dehlee, and built castles in the air upon the promises of my kind and worthy protector; these continued for some

months after his return home, when his most
lamented death put an end to my hopes, and
sealed my hard fate.   Despairing now of any
better result, I found it necessary to exert myself, and accordingly, with the small sum I had
saved, I began to trade; and thus I continued
from the year 1806 to 1808, when Mr. Seton,
then Resident at Dehlee, took me by the hand,
and renewed my hopes of better times.   He obtained for us the commutation of our pension into
jagheer, which by laying out a little money on
the land, and the exercise of much diligence, we
found capable of considerable improvement.   But
I had scarcely taken possession, and got interested
in my new employment, when in 1809 I was
summoned to head-quarters at Seharunpore by
General Hewitt, to whom Mr. Seton had recommended me, and who was assembling an army at
that place, to bring the Sikhs, who had become
turbulent, to a sense of their duty.   Here I met
with my old friend Colonel Worsely, who first
recommended that I should be put in command of
the Sikhs who were to join us, amounting to about
10,000 horse.

With this promise I went to Kurnaul, having
with me my 300 bargheers (stable-horse), who,

by the kindness of Lord Lake, had been put in
the civil service with the Resident of Dehlee,
and remained detached at Paneeput. The Sikhs,
however, came to terms, and gave up the point
we required, which was the establishment of a
station at Loodheana.

At this time, however, Abdool Sunnud Khan,
to whom Hansee and the district of Hurreeana
had been given in jagheer, being unable to manage
the country, was desirous to give it up; and I
was ordered to attend the Hon. Edward Gardner,
with my 300 sowars, on an expedition to settle it.
Through Colonel Worsely's means, my corps was
increased to 800 men with two gallopers, all intended for the Hurreeana district. In less than
two months I completed my number, for my old
comrades, who had gone to Ameer Khan and
Holcar, joined me as soon as they heard that I
had got again into favour. From 1809 till 1814,
I worked hard in the district, and performed with
my corps many acts of gallantry, as the whole
army can witness. Among others, I was at the
taking of Bhowannee, and in company with the
6th Native Cavalry charged the garrison who
were making their escape.*

* Detachment orders by Lieut.-Col. Ball, camp Bhowannee, 9th Sept. 1809.

In the year 1811, Skinner's warm friend, Mr.
Seton, left Dehlee to accompany the Earl of
Minto, Governor-General, on his expedition to
Java, and the following letter will serve to show
the esteem in which he was held by that excellent
man :—

On board the *Mornington*, 12th March 1811.

"My dear James,—My departure from Dehlee
was so very sudden, that I could not write to you;
even now I can scarcely find time to do so. I cannot, however, quit Bengal even for a *time*, without
requesting you to do me the justice to believe, that
my friendship for you will continue the same in whatever part of the world I may be; and that should it
ever be in my power to promote you or your brother's
views, I shall eagerly avail myself of it.

"Lord Minto is already well acquainted with your
merits ; in short, both of you stand high in the general estimation.   Remember me in the kindest manner
to your brother Robert, and tell him for me, that where-
ever I am, he must consider me his sincere *friend* and
agent. God bless you, my dear Skinner. Believe
me ever most cordially yours,

(Signed)   "A. Seton."

"P.S.—It is most gratifying to me to reflect, that

our friend Metcalfe, who succeeds me, feels towards your brother and you exactly as I do."

It seems that application had been made to Government at this time, to have the jaghire of the two brothers made hereditary, or revertible to their families after their own deaths; but this, as appears by a letter from the secretary to Government, to the Resident at Dehlee (C. T. Metcalfe, Esq.), the Governor-General in Council, notwithstanding the high esteem he professed to entertain for the Skinners, conceived it would be contrary to the principles on which jaghires were given to accede to, as being in effect equivalent to a perpetual tenure, and their request was accordingly refused.   But the estimation in which both were held, may be understood from the three general orders given at foot.*

* GENERAL ORDERS by the COMMANDER-IN-CHIEF.

Head-quarters, Camp Jheend, 4th Jan. 1813.

The Commander-in-Chief has seldom, on any similar occasion, derived greater satisfaction than from the review of the 1st battalion 19th native infantry, and Captain Skinner's corps of irregular cavalry, the whole under the orders of Lieutenant-Colonel Arnold, commanding at Hansee.

The performance of the battalion   *   *   *

—Of Captain Skinner's corps, the Commander-in-Chief

The services of the corps had, since their last formation, of course been restricted to local affairs, the reduction of refractory Zemindars, and such

considers it but justice to that officer thus publicly to declare, that the size, condition, and figure of the horses, and the arms, clothing, and appointments of the men, are of a superior description to those of any other class of irregular cavalry that have yet fallen under his Excellency's observation.

Acting in brigade, their movements indicated such a knowledge of European tactics as would enable the corps to combine, whenever required, its movements with those of regular troops; while its separate performance of the various movements more peculiarly appropriate to, and characteristic of, irregular horse, satisfactorily demonstrated the superior excellence of the corps for that line of service which is more immediately the object of its maintenance by Government.

The Commander-in-Chief requests Lieutenant-Colonel Arnold and Captain Skinner will accept his best thanks, for having, by their individual and united exertions, rendered the two corps at Hansee so highly disciplined and efficient.

(A true copy.)

(Signed)   A. GORDON,
                Deputy Adjutant-General.

———

DETACHMENT ORDERS by LIEUTENANT-COLONEL ARNOLD, commanding at Hansee.

29th Jan. 1813.

The commanding officer having, at the inspection, this

duty as arises in the settlement districts brought into order for the first time. But in the mean time, Lord Moira had succeeded Lord Minto as

morning, of the corps of irregular horse commanded by Captain Skinner, experienced singular satisfaction in the performances of their various evolutions, both regular and desultory, he begs to add his testimony to their extraordinary attainments in discipline, to those already awarded them by that experienced and veteran officer Lieutenant-Colonel Adams, whose sentiments were so fully acquiesced in, at the recent review of the troops, by his Excellency Lieutenant-General Champaigne.

Lieutenant-Colonel Arnold returns his most cordial thanks to Captain Skinner, for the result of his unwearied exertions so ably exemplified in the exercise this morning, and entreats he will explain to the corps at large the high ideas he entertains of their merits.

(Signed)   J. ARNOLD,
Lieut:-Col. commanding.

———

DETACHMENT ORDER by COLONEL ARNOLD,
commanding at Hansee.

6th Oct. 1814.

Colonel Arnold, in quitting the post of Hansee, where he has commanded for nearly three years, performs a grateful duty in returning his sincere thanks to Captain Skinner, for the great and prompt assistance, in all emergencies, received from him, Lieutenant Robert Skinner, and the corps of irregular cavalry, whose gallantry and good conduct has been repeatedly recorded. The orderly behaviour

Governor-General, and soon found that the prospect of more serious hostilities would demand an increase of military means to meet the emergency, and accordingly the following letter prepared Captain Skinner for employment more extensive and better suited to his zealous and active disposition :—

Camp Mooradabad, 6th December 1814.

(*Private and Confidential.*)

"MY DEAR SKINNER,—Instead of an addition of only four rissalahs, I am now to acquaint you, that the Governor-General is determined to augment the corps under your command to 3,000 sowars ; you may, therefore, proceed to take measures to raise that number as soon as you can, and let me know without delay what assistance you will require in money, that an advance may be authorized to enable you to carry the measure into effect.

"I wish you would let me know in confidence, what number of cavalry, of the same excellent descrip-

of the corps in cantonment, and the alacrity and effect with which they perform all duties required of them, cannot be surpassed. Colonel Arnold entreats of Captain Skinner to make known his sentiments to his brother, Lieut. Robert Skinner, and the corps at large, which he quits with regret, both as friends and valuable brother soldiers.

tion as that under your command, you could raise, and whether you do not think that raising a large body of them would probably have the effect of drawing off a great proportion of Meer Khan's best cavalry.—I remain, my dear Skinner, yours very sincerely,

(Signed)   " G. H. FAGAN."

The 3,000 horse were accordingly raised in less than a twelvemonth, and though the nature of the Nepaulese or Ghoorka war afforded but few and imperfect opportunities for the use of horse, small parties of this corps were attached to several of the detachments employed against the Ghoorkas, as at Kalunga and Jytock, with Generals Gillespie and Martindale, with Generals Nichols and Ochterlony, and they were eminently useful in assisting the regular troops in overawing the powers of Hindostan, especially Sindea and Holcar, who were looking anxiously to the event of our contest with the Nepaulese, and who, upon the unsuccessful opening of that war, shewed very significant symptoms of the spirit which animated them.

This increase of force, however, had reference not so much to the war at that time in progress, and in which cavalry could take but little part,

as to another and more important military enterprise, contemplated even at that time by the
Marquis of Hastings, and in which the services
of an efficient body of irregular cavalry, such as
Skinner's, were likely to prove most valuable. It is
obvious, in fact, that the noble Marquis did highly
appreciate the value of Skinner and his brother,
as commanders of such troops, as will appear from
two letters addressed by himself to that officer,
and which, though marked *confidential*, we scruple
not to annex at foot.*   Alas! all who could then

* LETTER from the MARQUIS OF HASTINGS to LIEUT.-COL.
SKINNER.

Futtehghur, 25th March 1815.

SIR,—Lieut.-Colonel Fagan has laid before me your letter
containing the application of your brother for leave to retire
from the service. Let me beg of you to entreat that he will
suspend his determination until he may be secure against
foregoing advantages which might have made the profession
agreeable to him. Circumstances have prevented my being
able yet (as I must carry the vice-president in Council with
me on such a point) to settle the rank for officers in the
irregular corps. I need not repeat to you my anxiety to
put that matter on a footing which would be gratifying to
officers of that description, and not much time is required
for arranging it.

You mention your readiness to sever from the corps which
you command a proportion which might make a separate
one for your brother. I own to you I should prefer his

have been interested in their being kept private, have long since ceased to think of earthly things, and the sentiments they express can but do honour

continuing (with advanced rank) second to you; though I would station him with a party of your corps at a distance from you. The wish to keep your command as respectable as possible, is what influences my disposition on that point. Therefore, tell me frankly whether your brother can be reconciled to that plan.—I have the honour, sir, to be, your very obedient servant,   (Signed)   MOIRA.

The MARQUIS OF HASTINGS to the same.

(*Confidential.*)

Futtehghur, 15th April, 1815.

SIR,—On reflection, I know not whether I have not to charge myself with omission, in not explaining to you (as it might have had weight with your brother) the particular bearing of the arrangement which I professed to have in contemplation. My motive, however, for the reserve was a just one. I wished to avoid the appearance of reckoning decidedly on the concurrence of Council on a matter which I had referred to their opinion, though I had expressed my own conviction to them of the expediency of the measure.

What I proposed was, to confer the qualified rank of lieutenant-colonel and major upon officers of talent and experience in the irregular service. You are sufficiently aware of the jealousy with which the opening such a door would be regarded by the officers of the regular army; therefore you will be sensible it was necessary to guard this first step with ostensible restrictions. Following the analogy which was fixed for the officers of the provincial corps of

to all parties.   There is another letter, however, that we shall insert here, as it happily expresses the high estimation in which Colonel Skinner was

Loyalists who served with the king's army in America, I proposed that the youngest major of the line should command the eldest lieutenant-colonel of irregulars; but that the field officers of the latter should command all captains of the regular service.   By this arrangement, you see, it would be practicable to entrust an irregular officer with a considerable force, having only the attention to place under him battalions which happened to be commanded by captains.   The degree in which such a capability of distinction must raise the situation of the irregular field officers will be obvious to you; and as I had contemplated the giving the rank of major to your brother, I naturally hoped the alteration might have made continuance in the service agreeable to him.   To give him the chance of availing himself of any variation in sentiment which this explanation might produce, I shall say nothing of his resignation until the answer from the Council shall arrive.   At the same time, it would be improper for me to keep him in suspense, if he still wish to abide by his determination; and in that case (but in that case only), his resignation shall be understood to have been accepted by me from the 10th inst.

You will comprehend that the rank to which I have alluded would not be progressive by ordinary brevet, though any brilliant service performed in it would actually tend to advancement.   Of course, these observations (though the outline merely is to be communicated to your brother) are intended to rest with yourself alone.   It will, I trust, be believed by you that I have peculiar pleasure in thus mani-

held by the most competent judges in the regular service.   It is from Colonel Worsely, formerly Deputy-Adjutant-General on Lord Lake's staff.

" MY DEAR SKINNER,—You will hear of the honour lately conferred on the Indian army by the Prince Regent, in allowing the officers to participate in the Order of the Bath.   Having had an opportunity of seeing the Earl of Buckinghamshire, by whom the measure was brought about, I observed to him, that if honorary members could be allowed on our side of the water, as had been done with regard to German and other foreign officers in his Majesty's service, that Captain Skinner, who commands a corps of irregular horse, possessed very distinguished claims to such notice.

" His lordship replied with readiness, that he had often heard of Skinner's corps ; but as he feared you did not hold any commission from his Majesty, he was sorry no such extension of the measure could be adopted.   I replied, you certainly had no commission from his Majesty, though you were now serving the

festing to a person so respectable and meritorious as you, the light in which I consider your equitable claims.—I have the honour, sir, to remain, &c. &c.,

(Signed)   MOIRA.

Hon. Company.   He then said the thing was impossible.

"Never mind, my friend, these things are only feathers, and at all events, no longer tickle us when once we pass the heyday of life, and exchange the tulwar for the zemeendary karkhanah, and at any rate, you may confidently indulge the reflection, that you have fully deserved this honour, though your nusseeb has not commanded or obtained it.   I must now conclude.   Believe me, yours very sincerely,

(Signed)   "H. WORSELY."

"Isle of Wight, 15th Feb. 1815."

The occasion which, as we have above remarked, gave rise to so great an increase of demand for irregular cavalry, as is pointed at in the letter of Colonel Fagan, was no less than the contemplated movement by Lord Hastings against the Pindarree freebooters and their supporters in Central India.

The consequences of that narrow and timid policy, which in 1805-6 huddled up a peace with the Mahratta states and powers of Central India, before they had been sufficiently humbled by our arms to feel their comparative weakness, and the necessity of an honest adherence to the treaties imposed upon them, very soon began to show themselves. In fact, a sense of utter impotence could alone restrain from action haughty chiefs, whose natural jealousy had been exasperated into hatred by defeat, and whose wounded honour and soreness of crippled power could only be soothed by the hope of one day turning upon their conquerors with better success than heretofore.

Of the principal Mahratta chiefs,—the Peishwah, Sindea, Holcar, and Bhounslah,—the first, forced into a subsidiary alliance by an impulse of self-preservation in a moment of danger, was again ungrateful; jealous of our interference, secretly hostile and treacherous. Sindea, though not an avowed enemy, still cherished a sullen hatred against the power that had humbled him, checked his course of conquest, and curbed his ambitious views. His secret enmity was discovered in the treasonable correspondence he maintained against the British interests, with the Nepaulese, with the Peishwah, and other ill-disposed chiefs. The hatred of Holcar and the Bhounslah had its origin in the same source; all desired our downfall as strangers and interlopers, who had placed a restraint upon their projects of devastation. Nor did gratitude for being delivered from the gripe of Ameer Khan restrain the hostile spirit of the last from acting against the power which had deprived him of Berar and Cuttack.

But, even had no hostility been evinced or suspected on the part of the Mahratta princes, the consequences of their system of government, or rather of misrule, were of themselves sufficient to call for interference on the part of the British authorities. Instead of discharging the functions of government by a system of regular departments, their only means for executing these duties lay in a lawless military force. Beyond the boundaries of his own immediate, and as it were personal domain, each chief collected what he could force from the people of the country at the point of the spear and by a system of forays; and the tribute thus collected was termed *chout*, or *moolkgeeree*, expressions equivalent to the black mail exacted by predatory bands in other countries. The country of Sindea, or Holcar, *never* enjoyed peace; its peasantry were never safe in person or in property. The army of these chiefs was constantly detached in parties under leaders, to raise contributions, to reduce forts, or punish refractory officers and zemindars, all over Rajepootanah, Malwah, and Bhopaul.

Such a system among the leading powers could not fail of encouraging that strong propensity to plunder so inherent in the population of all these districts; and, in fact, instead of making any attempt at putting down marauders, it became a part of the Mahratta policy to encourage such bands, for they afforded additional means to the protecting chiefs of enlarging their own sphere of military plunder. The consequence was, that, by the year 1814, the country was overspread with bands of freebooters, who ravaged, systematically, every district from the Kishna to the desert of Marwar.

It is by no means our purpose to inflict upon our readers a history of the rise and progress of these freebooters, who are best known by the name of Pindarrees. Those who are curious on the subject will find it very fully treated of in the authorities mentioned at foot.* It is sufficient to state, that in 1814 they were computed to have numbered full 40,000 horsemen of all sorts, without including those who attached themselves more especially to the armies of Holcar and Sin-

* J. Grant Duff's "History of the Mahrattas"; Sir John Malcolm's "Central India," vol. i.; Prinsep's "History of the Pindarree War."

dea, or the Patans of Ameer Khan, who, count-
ing horse and foot, is said at this time to have
been at the head of 30,000 men.

The principal leaders at this time were the following :—The celebrated Cheetoo, whose durra, or
horde, was estimated at from 10,000 to 15,000;
Kurreem Khan, at this time, only 4,000; Dost
Mahomed and Wasil Mahomed, 6,000; inferior
and independent leaders, 8,000.

Two sons of a famous chief (by that time dead)
named Burun, afterwards well known as the two
Rajuns, had not at this time acquired their full
influence, and generally acted with the other
sirdars.

These chiefs all haunted the valley of the Nerbudda, and the mountains to the north and south
of it. There they had their camps and strongholds, where, by sufferance of the fixed powers,
they bestowed their families and property when
absent on expeditions, and there they themselves
dwelt and pastured their horses during the rains
and hot weather. By the time of the dussera,—
an annual festival occurring at the end of October or beginning of November,—each chief planted
his standard in his camp, and to these flocked all
loose spirits and lawless adventurers who sought

to partake of their fortunes. There were formed their plans of rapine and plunder, and there they trained their horses for hard work and long marches. By the end of the dussera, when the rivers generally become fordable, they shod their horses, chose leaders, and set forth upon their projected *lubhur*, or foray. The party usually ranged from one to several thousands. Of these, the proportion of good and well-mounted cavalry was usually that of 400 out of every 1,000, and these were always armed with long spears and swords; besides which, every fifteenth or twentieth man had a matchlock. The rest were of all sorts, looties or common scamps, attendants, slaves, or followers of the camp, mounted as each man could manage, on tattoos or ponies, and armed with every sort of weapon they might possess. Thus, without baggage or encumbrances, their progress was so rapid as almost to mock pursuit; and the barbarous atrocities they committed, their ingenuity of tortures to extort property, and their system of wanton destruction were beyond the power of description.

Under such a progress of devastation, it is obvious that every country they visited must have become a waste, which grew wider and wider

as the mere exhaustion of its resources caused the
freebooters to spread further, until cultivation and
cultivators alike disappeared from the land. No
language can paint the melancholy scale of desola-
tion to which the Rajepoot dominions were reduced, and that of Meywar in particular; nor did
Malwah, Candeish, or the northern districts of the
Dekhan, Mahratta though they were, escape much
better. The sketch of a single lubhur, or foray,
which was made by Cheetoo, in the end of 1815,
upon the Company's territories, will suffice to give
some idea of the ruin effected by these miscreants
in a single season.

Mr. Prinsep tells us that the Pindarrees assembled at Cheetoo's camp, at the dussera of 1815, to
the number of 8,000 of all descriptions. They
crossed the Nerbudda on the 14th October, and
took a southward course. But soon breaking into
two masses, one, in passing the valley of the
Taptee, was surprised in its bivouac by a small
party of the Nizam's reformed infantry, under
Major Fraser. Galloping off, however, with but
little loss, they continued plundering in a southerly
direction to the banks of the Kishna.

The other party went to the south-east, and
passing through part of the Nagpore territories,

traversed those of the Nizam from north to south, as far as the bank of the Kishna; and the territories of the Madras presidency were only preserved by the accident of that river not being fordable at the time. The freebooters, therefore, turned eastward, marking their course by a broad line of fire and blood to the frontier of Masuli-patam; when they took a northward direction: and, eluding all the British posts and parties, returned along the line of the Godavery and the Wurda, to Neemawur. The booty acquired in the Nizam's dominions, in the course of this excursion, was so great, that there being no merchants of sufficient substance to purchase it at Neemawur, they had to send to Oojeine for purchasers.

This success led immediately to another ex-pedition. By the 5th February, 10,000 men, under various leaders, again assembled at Neema-wur, and crossing the Nerbudda, pursued the same track to the SSE. that had been taken by the former expedition on its return. And the first that was heard of this body was its appearance on the western frontier of the Masulipatam dis-trict in the Madras presidency, on the 10th of March. From thence it turned southwards, and next day made a march of thirty-eight miles, in

the course of which it plundered ninety - two
villages, committing in each the most frightful
cruelties. On the following day (the 12th), after
another march of thirty-eight miles, and the destruction of fifty-eight villages, the horde arrived
at the civil station of Guntoor, where they plundered all the houses of the civil offices, and a considerable part of the town.   The government
treasure, and the persons of the British residents,
were protected at the collector's office by the exertions of a few troops and invalids, kept at the
station for civil duties.   But Pindarrees never
risk loss either of time or life; so they decamped
immediately with what they could get, and before
night not a strange horseman was to be seen in
the neighbourhood.   The whole had hurried off to
the westward, making on the next day a march of
fifty-two miles.

For twelve days did this body of maurauders
continue pillaging within the Company's frontier;
and after leaving Guntoor, they swept through
part of the Kuddapa district, and recrossed the
Kishna on the 22nd of March—just escaping a
squadron of the Madras native infantry, which
came to the opposite bank at the very time they
had made good their passage.   Detachments were

sent out in all directions; but the lubhur split into several bodies, probably in order to baffle pursuit; and, though some of them had narrow escapes, the whole, or nearly so, of the large body that crossed the Nerbudda in February, had re-crossed it in safety by the 17th of May, having, with perfect impunity, carried off a second immense booty within the year. Of the damage done in the Company's territory in these twelve days, some idea may be formed from the report of a committee appointed to inquire into the whole matter; and from which it appears that, independent of the value taken or destroyed, there were 182 individuals put to a cruel death, 505 severely wounded, and 3,603 subjected to different kinds of torture.

Had this unequalled system of rapine and murder been confined to those provinces and states which the British, by their own mistaken policy, had placed beyond the pale of their own protection, even then so gross an injury to the prosperity of the whole country could never have been tolerated in its neighbourhood; but these daring acts of aggression upon its own territory and subjects, called imperatively for immediate punishment and measures of prevention for the future. And the Marquis of Hastings, fully aware of the intimate connection between the fixed and secretly hostile powers with the maurauders, resolved to adopt a plan of operations so extensive as at once to crush all such insidious hostility, and sweep from the face of the country every freebooter that infested it.

So early as the end of 1816, a number of detachments were thrown out from various points, with so much skill as to check the lubhurs of that season with considerable success, and great loss on the part of the Pindarrees. But arrangements on a far more extensive scale were in progress; and, while negociations were opened with those princes or chieftains who could be brought to reason, the preparations for coercing the refractory were silently but industriously carried on. During the summer and autumn of 1817, the various bodies of troops assembled at their posts. The grand army, under command of Lord Hastings in person, consisting of about 34,000 regular troops, was formed in three divisions and a reserve, and occupied positions at Agra, Secundra, near Kalpee, on the Jumna, and Kalinger in Bundelcund; the reserve being stationed at Rewarree south-west of Dehlee.

The army of the Dekhan, under command of Lieutenant-General Sir Thomas Hislop, was formed in five divisions and a reserve; and amounted to 57,000 regulars, which were disposed so as to cross the Nerbudda simultaneously at Hindia and Hoshingabad, to occupy positions in Berar and in Candeish, and act as circumstances should indicate; while a division from Guzerat was to enter Malwah by Dohud. To this large force of regular troops—the largest by far that ever took the field from British India—was added 23,000 of irregular horse, of which 13,000 were attached to the army of the Dekhan, and 10,000 to that of Bengal.

This vast scheme, rendered complete by some subsidiary details, was calculated to embrace the whole disaffected region; and advancing inwards, like one of Timour's or Chenghiz-Khan's gigantic hunts, to converge to any central point that should prove the fittest for final action, and thus gather together and crush, without hope of escape, every refractory or treacherous power within its circuit. Never, assuredly, was any plan of military operations better concerted to effect its purpose; and never was any combination of diplomatic and military tactics more completely crowned with

success. The end of that year, and the space of
a single month, saw the Peishwah and the Bhounslah, with the representatives of Holcar, baffled
alike in their intrigues and their efforts at open
resistance. The battle of Khirkee,* and its train
of consequences, sent the first a hunted fugitive,
worn out and driven alike from every stratagem
and stronghold, to a quiet asylum in the territories
of the power he had so shamefully abused. The
battles of Seetabuldee* and Nagpore, in like
manner, proved the deathblows to the Bhoun-

---

* We dare not trespass so far on the patience of our
readers as to inflict on them even the shortest sketch of the
three celebrated battles, which, if they did not actually ter-
minate, gave that spirit to the war which brought it to its
speedy issue—those of Khirkee, Seetabuldee, and Mehidpore
—although in the first of these 2,800 British troops, of
which only 800 were Europeans, broke and scattered 28,000
of the Peishwah's chosen troops; and, in the second, 18,000
Mahrattas and Arabs, brave and fierce soldiers, were repulsed
and put to flight by scarce 1,400 sepoys. That reply of
the gallant Fitzgerald, when, seeing the critical moment, he
repeatedly, but in vain, besought his commander for leave
to charge the cavalry which were swarming in the plain—
that reply will never be forgotten in India: "Tell him to
charge at his peril!" was the stern and impatient refusal he
received. "At my peril, then be it!" exclaimed Fitzgerald;
and dashing forward with his small party, all animated with
the same spirit, they scattered the immense body of horse,

slah chief; for though he did at first succeed in
deceiving the British authorities and obtaining
too favourable terms, his innate duplicity was not

took the batteries which were spreading death through our
ranks, and saved the day, and the life of every being on that
desperately contested ground.

Not less gallantly fought and dearly won was the battle
of Mehidpore, where Sir John Malcolm, who crossed the
river with scarce 2,000 bayonets, stormed and took seventy
pieces of well-served cannon in position, and routed 20,000
men. The desperate character of that single but conclusive
charge was attested by the loss, in one short quarter of an
hour, of nearly 800 men in killed and wounded.

Page after page might be filled with splendid traits and
anecdotes of these celebrated battles, did we feel a right to
diverge so far from the more special subject of this memoir.
But there is one exploit less known to the public, which, in
point of intrepid gallantry, may vie with any feat of this or
of former wars, and which we cannot pass over in silence.
It is that remarkable defence of Korreigaon by one weak
battalion of sepoys against an almost countless multitude.

Captain Staunton, in command of the 2nd battalion of
the 1st Bombay native infantry, had been summoned from
Seroor to reinforce the troops at Poonah, and had left the
former place 500 strong, with two 6-pounders, and twenty-
six European artillerymen, at eight on the night of the 31st
December. By ten o'clock on New Year's Day, after
marching all night, they reached the high ground above
Korreigaon, a village on the bank of the river Beema, from
whence they saw the whole of the Peishwah's cavalry,
25,000 horse, on the opposite side. Unable to ford the

long to be controlled or concealed.   He fled to
the Pindarrees, shared their ruin, and became a
homeless fugitive in a foreign land.

river in the face of this formidable force, Captain Staunton
took post in the village, which, though surrounded by a
low and ruinous mud wall, was entirely open on the east
side, and had numerous breaches towards the river side.
6,000 Arab and Ghossein infantry were called in by
the enemy, on the battalion making its appearance; and
scarce had it taken up its position, when 2,000 of these
advanced to assault it, under cover of showers of rockets.
They were gallantly met and repulsed at all points; but,
unfortunately, got hold and retained possession of a square
inclosure in the centre of the place, from whence they were
enabled to fire on the sepoys with deadly aim.   On the
first repulse, the village was instantly surrounded by swarms
of horse and foot furious to enter, and then began one of
the severest and most obstinately continued contests that
India ever witnessed.   The sepoys, fatigued with a long
night's march, without provisions or water, had to sustain the continued attack of myriads, constantly relieving
each other, and under a burning sun.   The ruinous wall
offered no protection—the enemy swarmed up to the very
guns.   Every foot of ground was disputed; several streets
were taken and retaken.   Half of the Europeans were
speedily killed or disabled; of the eight officers they had,
half were killed or wounded; and the Arabs, in successful
charge, having got possession of a small temple in which
three of them were lying, savagely murdered the wounded.
   The sufferings from thirst, especially of the wounded,
were now dreadful.   The men were either fainting from

The subjection of the once proud family of
Holcar cost even less time and trouble. Jesswunt Rao, after his return from the Punjab in

fatigue, or frantic for want of water, and seemed fast giving
way. At this moment, Lieutenant Chisholm, of the artillery, was struck down, and the Arabs charged and took one
of the guns. All seemed lost, when Lieutenant Thomas
Pattison—eternal honour to the hero!—lying there mortally
wounded, hearing of the loss of the gun, started to his feet,
and seizing a musket called upon the grenadiers to follow
him "once more." He rushed on the Arabs, striking to
right and left, and, well seconded by his men, scattered or
slew the Arabs, retook the gun, and then, again shot
through the body, fell upon the ground he had so nobly
won.

The headless trunk of Lieutenant Chisholm, dragged from
under a pile of dead Arabs, proclaimed to the men the fate
they had to look for, if the place should fall into the
enemy's hands. The slight success revived their spirits,
and one and all renewed the conflict; and although towards
evening nature again began to droop, and the situation of
the battalion was very hopeless, yet by nightfall the enemy
relaxed in their attack. The men got water. By nine
o'clock the firing ceased, and the village was evacuated by
the Peishwah's troops.

In the morning they were still seen hovering round the
village, and Captain Staunton opened his guns again, and
prepared for the worst. But they soon moved off in the
direction of Poonah, having heard of General Smith's
approach. Captain Staunton, not knowing this, resolved to
retire upon Seroor, but gave out that he still intended to

1806, survived for five years, in a state of moody and savage ferocity, that gradually lapsed into insanity. He died an imbecile madman in 1811.

His death, as is ever the case in such circumstances, was the signal for a perfect rush of crimes and intrigues of the most disgusting and revolting description, in which the fall or murder of the

continue his march to Poonah. Moving, as if with this intention, he suddenly counter-marched on Seroor, and reached that place next morning, carrying with him as many as he could of his wounded. His loss was 175 men in killed and wounded, of which twenty were of the European artillerymen. Of eight European officers, three were killed, and two wounded severely. During the action, the Peishwah, with the Satarah Rajah, sat on a height on the other side the stream, upbraiding his officers, and asked them, tauntingly, " where were now their boasts of defeating the English, when they could not overcome one battalion."

It is a singular and a touching trait of these gallant men, so far were they from priding themselves on this wonderful defence, that, mortified at not having accomplished the purpose of their march, and conceiving themselves beaten, they came into cantonments with drooping heads and a painful sense of humiliation ; nor was it until they experienced the hearty welcome and warm congratulations of their comrades that they were consoled and restored to their own self-esteem—they had, indeed, won a wreath of laurels which can never fade.—See a more detailed account of this glorious defence in Grant Duff's History, vol. iii. p. 435.

principal actors served but to clear the field for
a new succession of adventurers in the foul and
bloody work, and the whole country became a
scene of rapine and of pillage. In these crimes
and intrigues, the beautiful and infamous Toolsah
Bhye, the mistress of Jesswunt Rao, was the
principal actress; until her own time came at
length. She was separated from the young prince
Mulhar Rao, the nominal successor of Jesswunt;
and the very day before the desperate and deci-
sive battle of Mehidpore, she was taken from the
prison into which she had been cast by the then
dominant party, and brought, towards daybreak,
in her palankin to the bank of the Seepra. Many
were roused by her cries for mercy; " but no foot
was stirred, no voice was raised," said an eye-witness of the scene, " to save a woman who had
never shown mercy to others."

That battle broke, effectually and for ever, the
force and family of Holcar. Its guns were all
taken, its excellent infantry, many of them of
De Boigne's old brigades, were soon after destroyed; and at Murdissore, the submission of
the young chief was tendered to the British commander. On the 6th of January 1818, he entered into a subsidiary treaty, which reduced that

haughty house to the rate of a secondary state, and for ever put a stop to the mischief, of which their ambitious and intriguing spirit had so long been the cause.

Sindea, by good fortune, far more than by good policy or honesty, weathered the storm which destroyed his brother princes. Equally intriguing and deceitful; in correspondence with all the enemies of the British; the near vicinity of the army under Lord Hastings, and the division under General Donkin, kept him from moving until the battles of Khirkee and Seetabuldee opened his eyes, and he accepted the subsidiary treaty which, however distasteful, afforded him the only means of safety in his option.

The minor chieftains were easily dealt with. Separate treaties or settlements were made with each according to the nature of their respective cases; and above all, every state, large or small, in Central India and Hindostan, was guaranteed against the aggression of its neighbours or the incursions of predatory bands. Ameer Khan,—the chief of these freebooters, whose military establishment was such as to cause him to be regarded more in the light of a substantial power,—when he saw his former supporters all prostrated, all scope for future plunder cut off, felt that "his occupation was gone"; and though, with characteristic deceit and cunning, he fought for delay, he found at last that nothing remained for him but to submit to the terms of the conqueror. These were not hard; after many attempts at evasion, he gave up his guns, disbanded his Patans, some of whom were taken into the British service; and abandoning all schemes of ambition or of plunder, sat quietly down on his jaghire of Tonk Rampoorah guaranteed to him by British generosity, and worth 150,000*l*, a year.

With the states above mentioned, fell the Pindarrees; for them there was no longer any home or resting-place—their day was past. Of these chiefs, the famous Cheetoo, after a career of infinite variety and enterprize, embraced the fortunes of Appa Sahib; and after the battle of Nagpore, conducted the ex-rajah to the neighbourhood of Asseerghur, having had his followers cut up in detail by British detachments. An English party having made its appearance as he reached the vicinity of the place, his few remaining people dispersed, and he took refuge in the deep jungles of Egwâss. Unfortunately for himself, he would not trust in the promises of mercy held out by the English authorities; so here, wandering alone, tracked like a hunted animal by the hoof-prints of his horse, he was sprung upon and killed by a tiger. An officer of Holcar's, hearing of this event, hastened to the spot, where the horse, saddle, sword, ornaments and part of the body, with some papers, grants of land from Appa Sahib, were found. They traced the tiger to his den, and then discovered the head still perfect, and at once recognised it as that of the celebrated Pindarree Sirdar.

The fortunes of Kurreen Khan would furnish matter for a volume. At one time exalted, by a concurrence of fortunate events, to the semblance of independent power; at another, a captive in a dungeon, or a fugitive for his life, the year 1817 found him escaped from the camp of Holcar; and at the express desire of Sindea, joining the durra of Wâsil Mahomed to assist in opposing the English. But disappointed and disgusted at the refusal of that chief to assist them, from fear of detection by the British authorities, he abandoned his family, and fled, very slightly attended, back to Holcar's camp at Mundissore. From thence he was driven from similar motives to those of Sindea; and after concealment for some time, and under many disguises, he was persuaded at length to throw himself unconditionally on the mercy of the British government. By them he was sent to Goruckpore, where lands were allotted for his support. Namdar Khan, one of his chief leaders, also surrendered himself; and most of the rest followed his example. Wâsil Mahomed took refuge in Sindea's camp; but being seized and imprisoned there, in conformity with that prince's treaty with the British, he destroyed himself by poison.

Thus perished the Pindarrees, a growth of the diseased times—a race that could only have existed in an atmosphere of total anarchy and disorganization. Living solely on rapine, without any peaceful pursuit, it needed but to deprive them of all field for plunder, to effect their extirpation. To do this was the object of Lord Hastings in this extensive and complicated enterprize. How well he succeeded, we have seen. "There remains not a spot in India," says Sir J. Malcolm, "that a Pindarree can call his home. They have been hunted like wild beasts. Numbers have been killed; all who adopted their cause have fallen. Their principal leaders have either died, submitted, or become captives . .

A minute investigation only can discover any of these once formidable disturbers, concealed as they are amongst the lowest classes." Nothing, indeed, is more wonderful than the rapid fall and utter extinction of these marauders. All powerful and intangible as they appeared at the commencement of this striking campaign, before the year was out, they had vanished. In the month of September 1817, full one hundred thousand wild freebooters ravaged and trampled down the realms of Central India; by the end of December in the same year, they were gone—dead or merged in the peaceful mass of the people, never to reappear, leaving no trace behind them of the hordes that had desolated India. Such is one feat—one lasting and characteristic boon bestowed by the British government upon the people of Hindostan.

CHAPTER XV.

Operations of the reserve division of the army against Ameer Khan—Meeting of the Meer with Sir David Ochterlony—The Meer's appearance and conversation—Arrangement with him—Negotiations with Jeypore—Ineffective—Employment of Skinner's corps—Escort Bajee Rao to Bittoor, and Chimnajee, his brother, to Allahabad—General orders, and letters public and private—One-third of the corps paid off—A jagheer granted him in lieu of pension—Letters in regard to that arrangement—Further reduction of his corps —His observations thereupon—Narrative resumed—His corps again increased—Variously employed—Ordered to join the army at Muttra under Lord Combermere—March against Bhurtpore—Affair with the enemy—Major Fraser defeats a party of them, and takes possession of a disputed bund—Drives another party into the fort—General order —The corps volunteers to join the storming party—Shadull Khan's acceptance of his commander's charge—The mine sprung—The storm—Particulars of the various divisions—Gallant exploits—Major Hunter's encounter with a chief—The place taken—Degraded condition of the Bhurtpore state—Its reputed strength and riches—Chumars the depositaries of the secrets of hidden treasures—Settlement with Alwar, &c.—Entertainment given to Lord Comber-

IN the disposition of the troops for the campaign that has just been described, Colonel Skinner, with 2,000 of his corps, had been ordered to join Sir David Ochterlony, as part of the reserve division which was posted at Rewarree as a check upon Ameer Khan and his Patans. In the beginning of December, this reserve moved southward towards Jeypore, Ameer Khan being at that time employed in reducing Madhoo Rajepoora. Negociations were in progress with him, as well as with the Rajah of Jeypore: and it is a striking proof of how distasteful to all the chieftains of Hindostan was a treaty with the British, involving, as it generally did, a subsidiary force and some power of interference, that he could prefer the tender mercies of Ameer Khan and his Patans, who had been, and were still, ravaging his country, to the protection of the British government, clogged by such stipulations.

On the 10th, the reserve arrived at Sanganere, near Jeypore; whither vakeels came into camp from Ameer Khan. But the treaty with the Rajah made no real progress, and none of the officers were permitted to go into the town.

On the 15th, the treaty with Ameer Khan being in a state of forwardness, Sir David Ochterlony with his personal staff, Colonel Skinner, the Nawab Ahmed Buksh Khan, and some other persons, proceeded to a village four côs distant from the camp, in order to meet the Meer; who on his part advanced six côs from his own camp to see the General. The first meeting of ceremony took place next morning. The Meer was attended by 500 horsemen, a company of infantry, and two galloper guns. The parties came on elephants, and the Patan chief appeared to be under great alarm. When the elephants approached each other, in order that the General might take hold of the Meer's hand—the common salute under such circumstances—the attendant who sat in the howdah behind him, held a cocked pistol presented to the General's breast; and the horsemen were all prepared with lit matches, and carbines, and blunderbusses handled. After a hasty introduction, the Meer called out hurriedly, *" chulo, chulo!"* — " get on, get on," and they separated. The General, in a few minutes, retired to his tent, and Ameer Khan went to one pitched for him by Sir David's orders, he having brought none along with him.

In the evening, General Ochterlony visited the
Meer on business, and received the customary
presents; and next day visit and presents were
returned. It was remarked by the writer of this
account, that neither in appearance nor in address
did the Patan chief make any favourable impression. He was poor and mean looking, dressed
in a blue turban and dirty white upper garment.
He spoke but little, and what he said was trifling,
plebeian, and in bad style. He said that he was
king of Hindostan, but resigned his claim to it
from friendship for the General. His attendants
talked lightly of him, and abused him for truck-
ling, as they said, to the English, for which he
would get well handled on his return to camp.
His followers were not insolent, but fops in dress,
and ridiculous bullies in talking. Some of them
were handsome, respectable-looking soldiers; men
chiefly from Rampore and Mhow. The horsemen were well armed and mounted. There is no
doubt that the Meer's acquiescence in the treaty,
after all his evasions and subterfuges, was quick-
ened by the news from Nagpore and Poonah.
He had intelligence of these battles three days
before it reached the British camp: and he remarked that it was all nonsense to try fighting,

when two battalions could beat so many thousand men.

Notwithstanding the signature of the treaty, however, a final settlement with the Patan chief was not so close at hand. He was overawed by his turbulent troops, and instead of giving up his guns according to treaty, they were sent out along with his infantry to collect money in the Jeypore territory. At length, however, the mutinous state of his army, and still more, perhaps, the account which reached him of the total defeat and dispersion of Holcar's army at Mehidpore, forced him to a decision. He quitted his own camp, and came and pitched his tent within a mile of that of the reserve army. The General visited him next day, and sent him tents, camels, &c. " And now," continues the writer of this account, " he will lay himself up in ordinary, and enjoy twenty-two lakhs of rupees a year, the fruit of his treachery to Holcar, who had adopted him as a brother, and put his son into his arms to be to him as a child. While he was temporizing with the English, he was all along encouraging Guffoor Khan and Holcar's Mahratta chiefs to fight in the south. If they had succeeded he would have joined them; but since they have been defeated he stays where he is, and secures all his jaghires in Holcar's country, as a possession from the British Government for his son, and five lakhs in ready money for his useless guns. It was by his advice that Toolsah Byhe, one of Holcar's wives, was put to death before the late action, because she had agreed to come to terms with the English."

The writer may possibly be too severe upon the Meer in some part of these charges; for though there is no doubt of his strong propensity to intrigue and treachery, when it served his purpose, it is equally certain that if there was a redeeming point in the Patan's character, it was his long and almost faithful adherence to Holcar. When that chief died, and his family and court became a perfect hotbed of vice and intrigue, without any of the talent required to bring their ambitious designs to maturity, or to sustain the influence or power of the government, he may have fallen off from his allegiance; but then its object was no more, and he may have thought that none was left worthy enough, or safe enough, to cling to. He was a cautious, selfish, unprincipled chief; and, when the strong motive was gone, he acted up to his character.

Although Sir David, by a happy union of address

and firmness, succeeded at length in procuring the fulfilment of all the articles of the treaty, including the surrender of the Meer's guns, and the dispersion or absorption of his troops, the weak and vacillating government of Jeypore still held out, the only one of the Rajepoot states that had not embraced the terms of the British Government for receiving protection and support, and, therefore, the army of reserve remained still stationed in the neighbourhood of its capital. But Colonel Skinner, with his corps, was ordered to join a detachment under Colonel Patton, who was proceeding to Colonel Ludlow's force at Rampoorah. From thence, at the approach of Bajee Rao, he was summoned, with a thousand of his horse, by Sir John Malcolm; but before he could reach him the Peishwah had come to terms. With Sir John, at Mhow, he remained two months, when he was sent to escort Captain Low, in charge of Bajee Rao, to Bittoor, at which place he remained six months. In the course of these services, and, indeed, throughout the whole of this campaign, there occurred no opportunities for those displays of courage and gallantry, which enabled the corps to distinguish itself on former occasions; but that both corps and commander

acquitted themselves to the perfect satisfaction of
their superiors is amply attested in the annexed
letters.

"To LIEUTENANT-COLONEL SKINNER, Commanding
Irregular Cavalry.

" Head-quarters, Futtehghur, 20th May 1815.

" SIR,—The Right Honourable the Commander-in-
Chief must not omit to thank you for the zeal and
alacrity with which you proceeded against the refractory inhabitants of Bhowanee, on the 22nd April last,
and for the timely and judicious manner in which you
had previously detached the 200 sowars to the assistance of the police officers.   To these prompt measures
the Commander-in-Chief attributes the rapid suppres-
sion of the insurrection, and he has not failed to bring
the good conduct evinced by you and your corps on
this occasion, under the favourable notice of the
Right Honourable the Governor-General.

" The distinguished gallantry of Runjeet Khan, and
the four sowars mentioned by you, attracted his Excellency's particular notice, and he desires that his
thanks may be offered to that gallant officer and his
brave companions, for their meritorious services on the
above occasion.—I have the honour to be, &c. &c.

(Signed)   " G. H. FAGAN,
"Adjutant-General."

" DIVISION ORDERS.

" Camp, Mundissore, 20th Aug. 1818.

" Brigadier-General Sir John Malcolm cannot allow Lieutenant-Colonel Skinner's corps to leave the division without conveying to that officer, and through him to his officers and men, his sense of their uniform orderly and regular conduct. The Brigadier-General has been for many years familiar with the merits of Lieutenant-Colonel Skinner; his warmest wishes will ever accompany that officer, and the fine body of men under his command; and he trusts the latter will long continue to find, in a sincere and honourable attachment to their present leader, additional motives for the faithful and gallant performance of their duty to the government they serve."

———

" Mundissore, 20th Aug. 1818.

" MY DEAR SKINNER,—I have said and done no more towards you, than what a sincere regard for a warm, private friend, and a zealous servant of the public, dictated. A line was by mistake omitted in the order, which I have told Napier to correct. My right to express the feelings I have done in a general order, refer to my long acquaintance with your merits. I shall have great satisfaction in transmitting this tes-

timony to Lord Hastings, as an honest and sincere
tribute to one whom, in my opinion, he has done himself honour by patronizing in the manner he has done.

" Yours sincerely,

(Signed)   " JOHN MALCOLM."

———

" To LIEUTENANT-COLONEL SKINNER.

" Bittoor, 13th July 1819.

" SIR,—The Most Noble the Governor-General in
Council having decided that the services of the main
body of the troops under your command are no longer
required at Bittoor, I have the honour to request, that,
with the exception of one complete rissalah, which is
to remain under my orders for some time longer, you
will be pleased to place yourself and the corps under
the command of Major-General Sir Dyson Marshall,
from whom you will receive the requisite orders respecting your future movements.

" The sentiments I entertain of your public conduct, and of the uniformly correct behaviour of the
excellent corps under your command, since you have
been employed on your present duty, being fully stated
in my report of this date to Government, of which I
have the pleasure to inclose a copy for your information, I have little to add here, but to express my

anxious wishes for your health and prosperity, and that the fullest success may attend your exertions in every service on which you may be employed, and I beg to assure you, that the many obliging acts of private friendship which I have received from you, and the very cordial and useful aid which, during the last twelvemonth, you have rendered me in my official duties on all occasions, have excited feelings of esteem and gratitude which I can never forget, and have fixed in my mind the most sincere respect for your character, and the warmest interest in your welfare.

"I have the honour to be, &c. &c.
(Signed)   "JOHN LOW,
"Commanding with Bajee Rao."

The Report to Government alluded to in this letter, contains the highest encomiums on Colonel Skinner and his corps; but it is too long for insertion here, and merely repeats the sentiments expressed in Colonel Skinner's favour on other occasions, and is therefore omitted.

"EXTRACT DIVISION ORDERS by BRIGADIER-GENERAL
SIR JOHN MALCOLM, &c. &c.
Parole, *Seronge.*
"Camp, Mhow, 5th Feb. 1819.
"Brigadier-General Malcolm was much gratified

this morning, by the review of the 2nd Regiment of Skinner's horse, who are (as far as he can judge) exactly at that point of order and discipline most calculated to maintain their utility and efficiency, and promote the reputation they have acquired. Brigadier-General Malcolm had lately occasion to express his admiration of that part of this distinguished corps, under the immediate command of Lieutenant-Colonel Skinner. He cannot pay a higher compliment to Major Robert Skinner, his rissaldars and men, than by stating his opinion that the 2nd Regiment of Skinner's horse is equal to the first, not only in its discipline and appearance, but in those more essential principles of internal regulation, which maintain the character of a corps as high in times of peace as of war; by rendering it, from its good order and habits of regularity, a real protection to the inhabitants of the country in which it is employed. In this respect, every report Sir John Malcolm has received of Major Skinner's regiment since it entered Malwah has been the same, and it is one upon which he deems that officer and those under his command entitled to his particular praise and thanks."

(A true copy.)

"DETACHMENT MORNING ORDERS.

"Lieutenant-Colonel Smith cannot allow the attack made yesterday upon the Arab camp, however unimportant it may appear, to pass, without publicly recording his approbation of that event, the result of which reflects the greatest credit on the troops of the detachment. . . . . . .

"Lieutenant-Colonel Smith would be wanting in his duty, were he to omit on this occasion to express more particularly the high sense he entertains of the zealous and spirited conduct of Major Skinner, and the fine body of men under his command. The steadiness and alacrity with which they obeyed orders, the regularity of their rapid advance in two columns round the village where the enemy had been encamped a few hours before, and their subsequent gallant pursuit of the fugitives down the bypaths in the mountains, and the continuance of that pursuit to the very gates of Asseerghur, was such as would do honour to any corps, however exalted in character.

"The Lieutenant-Colonel cannot but express his admiration of the conduct of Skinner's horse, and requests Major Skinner will communicate those sentiments to the men under his command. It will be a part of the Lieutenant-Colonel's duty to bring to the notice of his superiors, the conduct of all the officers and men employed in these services.

(Signed)   " H. COYLE,

" Brigade Major.

" Camp at Kairee, 15th Feb. 1819."

A further general order, by Brigadier-General Malcolm, under date 26th of February 1819, upon Major Skinner leaving his command, speaks in the highest terms of that officer and his corps, and refers, in terms of the highest commendation, to the conduct of Major Skinner and his corps in the affair already described by Colonel Smith; but as the matter has already been given, it becomes unnecessary to repeat it.

There is, however, a letter written about this time by Sir John Malcolm to Colonel Skinner, which, containing as it does that distinguished officer's deliberate opinion not only of his corps in particular, but of the characteristic requisites of irregular corps in general, is too valuable to be omitted, and it is therefore given at length :—

" SIR JOHN MALCOLM TO LIEUT.-COL. SKINNER.

" Mhow, 23rd Dec. 1819.

"MY DEAR SKINNER,—I should sooner have answered your letter, inclosing your reply to the 'Bengal

Cavalry Officer.' Calumnies upon corps or individuals have on some occasions their uses, when they elicit that truth from modest merit which gives publicity to actions that should never be forgotten. This has been the case on the present occasion. The plain and admirable statement you have given of these affairs—which the brain of the 'Cavalry Officer,' anxious to establish some favourite hypothesis, confused and misrepresented—will do you and your corps the greatest credit. You can both boast, that though there was in an hour of extreme trial some defection, never was the honour of a body of men better vindicated, than by the exemplary punishment (inflicted by the corps itself) of the criminal cowards who deserted their standards.

"The 'Bengal Officer' should have thought more before he alluded to a partial defection of a few of your men, a solitary instance of desertion; and tried on that ground to stigmatize a class. But he is, I understand, dead; and let the subject, which the imprudence of friends has used his name to revive, die with him. It will be more gratifying, and more salutary, to allow our minds to dwell upon the numerous instances of heroic valour and unshaken attachment that distinguished both the regulars and irregulars of that fine army, which, commanded by

our noble friend Lord Lake, conquered Hindostan, than to expose the failings of deceased worth
by groping amidst old posthumous MSS. for produc-
tions probably repented of as soon as written. But
with a man who has a purpose to serve, and an editor
who has a page to fill, much less consideration is,
I fear, given than ought to be to the feelings of
others. Letters, however, like that you have sent
to the journal, are calculated to do great good.
Unless there is bad intention (and I acquit the parties of that), they will learn caution when they see the
effect such attacks upon individuals and corps produce.

"I am glad you propose to give a short memoir of
your corps. If written, as I have no doubt it will be,
with the same clear conciseness, and in the same
spirit of modesty and truth, which it no doubt will
be, that marks your letter to the Calcutta journal,
it will be a most valuable document. With respect
to the merits of our irregular horse, you know my
sentiments. We have, both in our own services and
as auxiliaries, many excellent bodies of this class of
soldiers. Yours are the best I have seen of the
former description, though I believe some of the
Rohilla corps are very good; but yours have had
great advantages, and have made admirable use of
them. I do not mean to flatter, when I say you

are as good an Englishman as I know; but you are also a native irregular, half born and fully bred; you armed them, understand their characters, enter into their prejudices; can encourage them, without spoiling them; know what they can and, what is more important, what they *cannot* do. The superiority of your corps rests upon a foundation that no others have. Your rissaldars* are men, generally speaking, not only of character, but of family; those under them are not only their military, but their natural dependants. These are links which it is difficult for the mere European officers to keep up. They too often go upon smart men; promote, perhaps, a man of low family and indifferent character among themselves for some gallant actions; and then ascribe to envy, jealousy, and all unworthy motives, the deficiency in respect and obedience of those under him; forgetting the great distinction between regular and irregular corps in this point. Your personal kindness and generosity to your corps, has also effected much : and I have even found in Hindostan, fourteen years ago, and in Malwah during the last two, that every horseman of your corps considers, whether his duty requires him to act against the enemy, or to

* Native captains of troops. A *rissalah* is generally a troop of 100 men.

protect the inhabitants, that he has "*Sekunder Sahib-Ke-Aĥoo*" in his keeping.   This, I delight in observing, is a master-motive with them on all occasions.

"To conclude with my opinion upon irregular horse. Independent of the policy of keeping in pay, or in the service of our allies, a considerable number of this class, I know not, on the scale we now are, how we can operate in the field without them; but everything depends on their good management.   They are no more fit for the duties of regular cavalry than the latter are for theirs.   They are our light troops; and as such have their distinct place: to take them out of that is their ruin.   You know my opinion; that you have gone to the *very verge* of making bad regulars of admirable irregulars.—Yours, ever sincerely,

(Signed)   "JOHN MALCOLM."

Nor was the younger Skinner a whit behind his brother in rendering himself useful and acceptable to his commanders during this stirring period.   Immediately after the rains, he was ordered by Sir John Malcolm to join Colonel Smith, then in command of a detachment from the Madras presidency; and he distinguished himself in the pursuit of Appa Sahib, the ex-Rajah of Nagpore, cutting up his people, with a small party of his sowars, to the gates of Asseerghur. And, in the beginning of 1819, he escorted Chimnajee, the brother of Bajee Rao, to Allahabad, under command of Captain Clarke; for both of which services it will be seen that he received the thanks of his commanding officers.

With this war, commonly called " the Pindarree war," the active military career of Colonel Skinner may be said to have closed. There was, in fact, no longer any field for active service on any considerable scale in Upper India. Accordingly, at the close of 1819, one-third of Skinner's corps was paid off; the second, under Major Robert Skinner, was sent to Neemuch; while the remaining 1,000 men, with the Colonel himself, continued at their old quarters of Hansee.

In the mean time, one of the favourite objects of Skinner's desire was accomplished, in the grant of the small estate he had hitherto enjoyed in his jaghire being made perpetual to his family. It was an act of bare justice, a mere redemption of a former pledge; but the manner in which it was done reflected credit on Lord Hastings, while conferring a benefit on its object; to whom the information was conveyed in the following letter from the secretary to Government :—

" To LIEUTENANT-COLONEL SKINNER.

"SIR,—It having come to the knowledge of the
Governor-General in Council, that you are solicitous
to secure, as a provision for your family, the perma-
nence of the grant of the jaghire held by you in the
district of Alleeghur, in commutation of your pension
as an officer retired from the service of the Mahratta
states, his Excellency in Council has not hesitated
on resolving to grant the jaghire to you and your
heirs in perpetuity; desiring, by this public mark of
favour, to acknowledge and to remunerate your distinguished merits and firm attachment to the British
Government, which, throughout a long period of
honourable and active service, have been uniformly
conspicuous.

" Conceiving that it may add to your satisfaction, as
well as be in itself a just reward of very considerable
merit, the Governor-General in Council has been
further pleased to resolve to grant, in perpetuity, to
your brother, Major Robert Skinner, and his heirs,
the small jaghire which he holds in the district of
Alleeghur, in commutation of his pension as a Mahratta officer. You are requested to communicate this
resolution to Major Skinner.

" I am directed to inform you that the necessary

orders will be issued to the proper local authorities
for giving effect to the arrangements of which I have
now had the honour to apprise you.—I have the
honour to be, &c. &c.,

(Signed) " J. ADAM,

" Chief Sec. to Government."

" Fort William, 26th Sept. 1818."

The following letters also show the feelings
with which the Colonel's most attached friends
learned his good fortune :—

" Camp, Mhow, 6th Oct. 1818.

" MY DEAR SKINNER,—I have great pleasure in
giving you the following paragraph of a private letter,
this morning received, from Adam.

" ' Your friend Skinner's jaghire will be confirmed
to him and his heirs. He well deserves it, and your
eulogy of him is not a bit overcharged.'

" One of our best Persian songs has a chorus—

' Allee Shah-in-shah Moobarik bashud ! '

In sober English, I wish you joy, and feel most
warmly to Lord Hastings for his just understanding
of your character.—Yours, ever truly,

(Signed) " JOHN MALCOLM."

"15th Nov. 1818.

"MY DEAR SKINNER,—I cordially congratulate you on your good fortune, for which you are indebted to the kindness of Lord Hastings, and your own merits, which have powerfully recommended you to his favour. Believe me sincerely joyful at your success, and ever yours, most truly,   (Signed)   "C. T. METCALF."

———

"DEAR JAMES,—It was not that I did not receive great pleasure from your communication, but because I was unwell, and for some time past unable to write, that it has been so long unacknowledged.

"I rejoice very much in the complete accomplishment of your wishes; but, valuable as the gift is, I think it has been made much more so by the very handsome terms in which it has been bestowed, and that you may long live to enjoy, and to continue to deserve, such kindness, is the sincere wish of yours, sincerely,

(Signed)   "D. OCHTERLONY.

"Camp, 30th Nov. 1818."

On the death of his brother Robert in 1821, Colonel Skinner's corps suffered a further reduction; Major Skinner's division being made over to another officer, Colonel Baddely; but we shall give the winding up of the original memoirs in the author's own words.

"I was, however, still at the head of 1,200 horse; and in 1822 I went to Calcutta, where I was very kindly treated by Lord Hastings. He promised that he would not lessen my command by a single man; but no sooner had he left the country than my corps was at once reduced to 800 men. Rapid, indeed, has been my fall. In the Mahratta service from 1796 to 1803, I had always a well-grounded hope of rising in rank and fortune; no question was ever raised as to my birth there. When I entered the British service, I believed that I gained a field in which the fruits of zeal and fidelity would be matured and reaped in perfection; and no exertions on my part were spared to forward this object. I imagined myself to be serving a people who had no prejudices against caste or colour. But I found myself mistaken. All I desired was justice. If I was not to share in all the privileges of a British subject, let me be regarded as a native and treated as such. If *I was* to be regarded as a British subject, did the hard labour and ready service of twenty years merit no more than a pension of 300 rupees per month; without either rank or station? and after

the distinct and repeated promises of the permanent
maintenance of my corps, was it fair that I should
be left liable to be commanded by the youngest
subaltern in the army, deprived of the hope
which I had so fondly entertained of passing my
old age tranquilly in that service to which my
better years had been devoted?　But I thank my
Creator that there remains one source of satisfaction—one consolation under every disappointment; and it is this,—that I have ever discharged
my duty as a soldier with honour and credit;
that during the space of twenty years, in which
I have served with Europeans, no one can ever
upbraid me with dishonouring " the *steel*," or being
" faithless to my salt"; that, finally, though I
have failed in gaining what I desired and deserved,—that is, *rank,*—I have proved to the world
that I was worthy of it; by serving my king and
my country as zealously and loyally as any Briton
in India."

If any reader should regard the tone of sadness
and disappointment which prevails in this perora-
tion as unreasonable or misplaced, let it be observed that much allowance should be made for
the circumstances of Skinner's peculiar case.　It
may at first sight appear that the " full retiring

pay of a lieutenant-colonel in the Company's service" was a liberal provision for all that Colonel
Skinner could have done in a three years' service;
for no longer had he served when this was first
granted to him. But this would be a very partial
and imperfect view of the case. For regard must,
in the first place, be had to the reasonable hopes
of advancement in rank, and provision for the
future, he had in the Mahratta service, as was
demonstrated by the fortunes which many Europeans made in it, and which he was *forced* to
abandon. In the next place, he might reasonably
pitch his expectations high, when he saw traitors
and deserters receiving splendid allowances; and
even his own native officers pensioned with 5,000
rupees a year each. But he entered the British
service without any sordid views, and with all the
enthusiasm of a generous mind, increased by an
admiration for his first commander. He had been
encouraged by the commendation and the volun-
tary promises of that commander — promises
addressed still more to his thirst for military rank
and honour, than to his interest. Honest and true
himself, he could not but believe that the faith
kept with the treacherous and the cowardly, would
be equally sacred towards the zealous and the brave.

Had even the pittance bestowed upon him been accompanied by military rank, it would have fulfilled his most ardent expectations; but when his birth was brought up as a misfortune, if not a reproach, and, like a two-edged blade, was made to cut both ways against him, it is scarcely to be wondered at if he became indignant at what looked very like a pitiful subterfuge for denying him that right to honour and reward which had been conceded and established by so many spontaneous declarations and promises in the highest quarters.   It is also to be held in mind that Skinner, at the time when this was written, had not even imagined the honours which were hereafter to be wrung from the tardy justice of his country, by the powerful and reiterated representations of his many and noble friends; and we venture to say that few men, if any, in India could boast of having won so bright and distinguished a succession of hearty friends as James Skinner; and of this the correspondence which we have already given, as well as some letters we still mean to offer to the reader's notice, is a sufficient proof.   At a subsequent period, this narrative was continued; and it is from this continuation that we shall now proceed with our work.

From the last-mentioned period,—that is, about the end of 1822 till 1824,—nothing occurred worth recording; nor, in fact, was the corps employed in that year, in any more serious service than that of suppressing the outbreaks of certain troublesome zemindars, chiefly in the Bhuttee country; and in driving from thence a troublesome freebooter, or *cazak*,* named Soorjah, a Rajepoot chieftain, who had gathered together a band of armed robbers amounting to near 5,000 men, it was said, and who did some damage before the force sent after him could overtake him.

On the Colonel's return to Hansee from this expedition, he, however, was greeted with a very pleasing piece of intelligence. This was a resolution of Government to replace under his command another corps of horse equal to that he then had. I lost no time, says Skinner, in promulgating this good news; so that all my old men, who, to use their own phrase, "had been praying for such a day," flocked around me; and in the course of a month and a half, I mustered my new corps, equipped, complete and efficient, in all respects, men and

* Robber, freebooter—probably derived from, or having a common root with, the name of the Tartar tribes, called Cossacks.

M 2

horses; and immediately commenced drilling
them. Shortly after I received orders to complete both corps from 800 to 1,000 men each.
And this enabled me to admit many more of my
veteran soldiers who had been disbanded, while
the new appointments and promotions were filled
up by seniority with men who had distinguished
themselves by their gallantry.

Two months after this augmentation, I was
reviewed by General Reynolds, who also presented colours to the corps with the usual ceremonies; and issued a very flattering general
order respecting the appearance and performance
of the men. In the evening, we gave him a
grand English and Hindostanee entertainment;
and he left the station much pleased and gratified.
Soon after, I was directed to recruit 400 horse
for Captain Hawkes, and a similar number for
Colonel Gardiner, both commanding corps of
local horse. This I did in a short time; and sent
them well equipped in every respect to their
respective commandants.

In 1825, the state of affairs in the Jhat states
of Bhurtpore and Deig called again for the interference of the British authorities. Since the
death of Rhundeer and Runjeet Sing, the chiefs

of Lord Lake's day, the court had become a
scene of intrigues and debauchery which produced
the greatest disorder.   At length Doorjun Lal,
the uncle of the young Rajah Bulwunt Sing, confined his nephew, and usurped the throne; at the
same time his arrogance was such as to draw on
that punishment from the British Government
which had long been due to that turbulent state.
An army was accordingly ordered to assemble at
Muttra early in the year, under command of Sir
David Ochterlony; but, from some change of
policy or plan, it was broken up until the ensuing
cold weather, when it again assembled under the
command of Lord Combermere, then commander-
in-chief.   Of this army, Skinner's horse was
ordered to form a portion.

We arrived, says Skinner, (the 1st corps) at Muttra on the 28th November, where his lordship and
Sir Charles Metcalfe soon joined us. Immediately
after his arrival, Lord Combermere inspected my
corps, and expressed himself greatly pleased.
" He had frequently heard of the corps," he said,
" and never but in terms of praise; and yet, what
he witnessed at the inspection exceeded every
expectation he had formed." The men, to whom
I fully explained the sentiments thus expressed

by his Excellency, felt proud indeed at having thus, at the first inspection, gained the applause and esteem of so gallant a British cavalry officer.

All preliminary arrangements for the siege having been made, Lord Combermere ordered one-half my corps (500 rank and file), under Major Fraser,* my second in command, to join the Agra

---

* This gentleman is the same who has already been mentioned as Skinner's most intimate friend. He was also the writer's brother, and it is not without some feelings of hesitation that he brings him so prominently forward in the narrative. His appointment, in fact, was a curious and anomalous one, and therefore may claim a few words of explanation. Mr. Fraser had, at a very early period, had much to do with Skinner's corps. It was by their aid that he had brought under control the district of Mewatt and other very wild and refractory ones in the "assigned territory"; and during the Ghoorka war, in which he was political agent with the army, under General Martindale, and made several long and hazardous journeys amongst the mountains in the prosecution of that duty, he was constantly attended by a detachment of this corps. After the war, being appointed commissioner for the settlement of the Hill states, he found not only the military escort, but the military character, of so much use in bringing these wild countries into order, that he made it a plea for urging, what assuredly was not disagreeable to his own tastes—for he was by nature far more of a soldier than a civilian—the expediency of investing him with military rank, as the best means of aiding the objects of his mission. To this Lord Hastings, enterprising

division of the army (with which it served throughout the siege), under command of Sir Jasper Nicholls; while his Excellency himself assumed that of the Muttra division; and both moved from their respective stations towards Bhurtpore, on the morning of the 10th December. On our second march, the day of our arrival before that place, my corps, supported by a squadron of H.M.'s 11th light dragoons, and another of native cavalry, with some light infantry and gallopers, was ordered to form the advance guard of the army; and had received orders to march, direct, and take possession of the water *bund* from which, on occasion, the ditch of the town was filled; but on entering the heavy

and chivalrous himself, and willing to gratify a congenial taste in an officer who had already done his work well, gave him the option of receiving the *local* rank of Lieutenant-Colonel, unattached to any corps, or that of Major, and second in command to the corps of his friend Colonel Skinner. He did not hesitate a moment in choosing the latter, which gratified Skinner as much as himself; and till the day of his death he held that rank, led his corps wherever it was ordered on service, and bore the brunt in every affair they were engaged in. At other times he was the civilian, and discharged the duties of chief commissioner in the ceded and conquered provinces, we believe, with unquestioned efficiency.

jungle before Bhurtpore, we went straight towards the fort instead of the bund, which lay quite in an opposite direction. A troop of mine was thrown out in advance as skirmishers; and as we had got pretty near the ditch, a slight skirmishing commenced with a body of the enemy's horse, who were advancing apparently to attack us.

On seeing this, General Reynells immediately ordered our troops to form. The gallopers, under that distinguished veteran Colonel Starke, first drew up and unlimbered; and I could not help admiring the cool steadiness of this fine detachment of artillerymen, as they stood to their guns, anxiously awaiting to welcome the enemy's approach with a salvo of grape. The infantry formed on the right, and my corps was directed to deploy into line on the left of the gallopers. But the enemy seeing us thus on the alert, retired; on which the fort immediately commenced a heavy cannonade; and as we had well got under their range, so that several casualties occurred, General Reynells ordered a retreat; but we halted when out of reach, and remained under arms until the whole of the army had come up and encamped.

When our retreat was sounded, Colonel Stevenson, quarter-master-general, with his usual coolness and gallantry, rode straight up to the bund, accompanied only by a few of his hircarrahs and a small party of pioneers, under command of Captain Irvin of the Engineers. On reaching it, they found the place completely evacuated by the enemy, and in possession of Major Fraser, who had taken it. The enemy had only just opened it; and Captain Irvin immediately commenced stopping up the mouth of the water-course, so that the ditch remained dry during the whole siege. On information of the affair of the bund being received by General Reynells, he immediately proceeded thither with some infantry, and took possession of a garden upon the bank of the Jheel, which he set instantly to work on and stockaded.

After the army had encamped, some of my men brought me word that Major Fraser, with his detachment, had had a brilliant affair with the enemy; and thus gained the honour of the first engagement before Bhurtpore. Major Fraser, supported by some of the regular troops, formed the advance-guard of the Agra division. They also had received orders to proceed direct to the bund: and on coming up, found a large encampment of the enemy's pitched close to the garden;

under the command of Neem Ranah Rajah, who
had joined the Bhurtporeans, and had "sworn to
his colours" that he would remain out to guard
the bund, and have the first encounter with the
British force.   On seeing Fraser's detachment
appear unexpectedly, they got confused; and on
being charged, fled to the fort.   Fraser gallantly
pursued them up to the very glacis; and so very
closely and determinedly were they followed,
that the enemy shut the town gates against their
own men, for fear that ours might force their way
in with them.   The Rajah being a brave man,
however, and seeing no other alternative left,
called out to his men to rally; and leading them
himself, charged gallantly back.   He fought desperately; but being soon slain by my men, his
followers lost courage and either fled into the
jungle or surrendered.   The loss on our side was
about twenty rank and file killed and wounded;
among the latter was Fraser himself, who received a
slight spear wound in the face.   That of the enemy
was much more considerable; and a number of their
horses, arms, &c., were captured by our men.

On the following morning, Fraser's detachment
was again ordered out upon a foraging party; and
having been desired to charge some of the enemy's

horse standing near the fort, the detachment galloped right up to the ditch; but the enemy would not wait to receive them, and retired into the fort, which immediately opened a smart fire on our detachment. The firmness displayed by Fraser in his retreat—not permitting the men to go out of a walk—surpassed every idea I had formed of his gallantry; and though the shots began to tell severely on the column, I was glad to learn that both on this and the preceding occasion the men behaved with most unswerving steadiness. Indeed, they could not well have done otherwise, with the gallant example of their leader in their view; and right glad I was that they proved themselves not unworthy of being placed under so brave an officer. The casualties on this and the preceding engagement were, ten rank and file killed, and twenty wounded, besides fifteen horses; and so close did they approach the fort, that the bodies of five or six of my men were left upon the glacis.

During the siege, the whole of my corps was constantly employed on escort and forage duties, as also in furnishing pickets, &c.; and in repeated instances did detached parties distinguish themselves, and by their gallant conduct elicit the applause of his Excellency the Commander-in-Chief, as may be seen by referring to the Adjutant-General's letters. *   His Excellency finding the first corps so useful, ordered my second corps, then stationed at Hansee, to be relieved by Captain Hawkes's corps, the 7th local horse, and to join the army at Bhurtpore. But it only came latterly, as, during most part of the siege, it remained as a corps of observation at Dring, a place

* The following is an extract from General Orders, by the Commander-in-Chief.

"Head-quarters, Bhurtpore, 21st Jan. 1826.

" The services of the 1st and 2nd corps of irregular horse, under command of Lieut.-Colonel Skinner, assisted by Major Fraser, throughout the siege, have frequently elicited the highest admiration and applause. Nothing could exceed the bravery of this valuable class of soldiers; and Lieut.-Colonel Skinner and Major Fraser fully merit this acknowledgment of his lordship's unqualified approbation of their conduct, and that of their men."

The conduct of two rissalahs employed on forage duties, under Rissaldars Amanut Khan and Zubberdust Khan, in beating off upwards of 1,000 of the enemy, commanded by several sirdars of note, and completely routing them, is acknowledged in terms of high encomium by the Adjutant-General, by his lordship's command. As is also the gallantry of Rissaldar Meer Bahaudur, who, with a piquet of the corps, charged and beat off a party of the enemy of 250 men, with the loss of thirty men killed and ten horses taken. The documents themselves are omitted being too voluminous.

between Deig and Bhurtpore, to watch the conduct of Madhoo Sing, the Deig Rajah, who, though openly declaring himself an ally of the British, was supposed to be secretly aiding and assisting the cause of his brother, Doorjun Lal, the usurper of Bhurtpore.

His Excellency having ordered a storming party to be formed of dismounted volunteers from the cavalry, my corps was directed to furnish 200 men for that duty. When I made known this order, and called out for volunteers, the whole corps replied, that if any selection was to be made, they wished me to do it myself, as, if left to their choice, they would all go. This praiseworthy spirit left me no alternative. To avoid hurting the feelings of any one, I refrained from all selection; but ordered the party to be told off agreeably to the "roster of duty"; but as I wanted a steady and experienced commandant to lead them, I placed at their head Shadull Khan, one of my oldest, most faithful, and trustworthy native officers; and on the evening previous to their joining the detachment of cavalry volunteers, I paraded this fine party, and thus addressed them :—" This is the first time of your going into danger when I cannot accompany you; but such is my affection for you all, that I cannot allow you to part from me without carrying with you something dear to me." Then, taking by the hand my son James, whom, on the late augmentation, Government had permitted to enter my corps as adjutant, I went on—" See, here is my son! take him, and gain for him such laurels as you have won for the sire."

On this the noble Shadull Khan, of whose valour I had often been an eyewitness, stepped forward, and taking my son by the arm, called aloud, in reply,—" Farewell, our own commander, trust in God, who never deserts those faithful servants who do their duty; and who, please God, will now do their utmost to maintain the honour of the corps." Having said this, the whole party gave three cheers, and went off to join the camp of the volunteers, while I and the rest returned to our lines with tears in our eyes.

The storm, however, was deferred, and the Company's European regiment having arrived, the cavalry volunteers were ordered to join their regiments before it took place. But both the Commander-in-chief and Brigadier Sleigh, who commanded the cavalry division of the army, issued very handsome orders on the spirited manner in which the cavalry had volunteered their services for the storm.

The engineers having reported the grand mine " ready," and the breach " practicable,"* his Excellency ordered the storm on the morning of the 18th January. His orders were speedily carried round the camp, and before daybreak all the infantry corps destined for the storm moved into the trenches, and the cavalry were detached all round the fort to prevent escape. The following was the plan of attack:—

* When the breach was first reported practicable by the engineer officer, Lord Combermere asked Skinner, who was by, his opinion on the subject; to which he only replied that he was unworthy to touch his Excellency's shoe, much more so to offer him advice. But his lordship, desirous of learning his opinion, repeated the question, and urged a reply. On which Skinner said that the breach was impracticable, and that, if attempted, the men would sink up to their armpits in the rubbish, and there would be a repetition of the former failures. Colonel ———, then a subaltern in the engineers, said he differed, but would ascertain the fact, and gallantly rushed forward, crossed the ditch, and found that it was as Skinner had stated. He returned untouched by the fire, patted Skinner on the back, and said, " Old boy, you are right and I am wrong." Skinner then said they must just do as the Mahrattas used to do on similar occasions, and trust to mining. They did mine, and the event proved the soundness of his opinion.

The right column was directed to escalade the breach, close to the Juggernaut gate, and consisted of two companies of the European regiment, the 58th native infantry, under Captain J. Hunter, and 100 ghoorkas, the whole under command of Colonel J. Delamaine.

The main column for the assault of the cavalier breach, under the immediate orders of Major-General Reynells, consisted of Brigadier Paton and McComb's brigades, which were to form two columns; and, after gaining possession of the breach, were directed to file up to the right and left.

A column of reserve, under Brigadier Whitehead, was left at the head of the trenches, and consisted of two companies of his Majesty's 14th, the 18th and 23rd regiments of native infantry.

The left main column was placed under the immediate orders of Major-General Nicholls, and consisted of Brigadier-Generals Edwards and Adam's brigades, with a column of reserve.

An intermediate column, consisting of two companies European regiment, and grenadier companies of 35th native infantry, light company of the 37th regiment, and 100 ghoorkas, all under command of Lieutenant-Colonel J. Wilson, was directed to escalade the angle of the long-necked bastion between the two main columns.   The springing of the mine under the north-east bastion was the signal for attack, and to this quarter every eye was anxiously directed.

The explosion took place exactly at eight o'clock, when it is supposed that the greatest part of the enemy destined to defend *that* point were blown up.   The grenadier company of the 14th also suffered materially from the explosion, having been advanced to the foremost point in the trenches, close to the bastion.   Brigadiers McComb and Paton, Lieutenant Irvine, of the engineers, and Lieutenant Daly, of his Majesty's 14th foot, were most severely wounded, and carried off; the latter officer had his leg amputated on the spot.

As soon as the dust had subsided, that brave officer Major Everard was the first who moved forward, gallantly leading his Majesty's 14th up to the breach.   Major-General Reynells immediately followed, and a momentary hesitation on the part of the sepoys being remarked at this critical time, the General gallantly stood up on the summit of the bastion, exposed to the heavy fire from the citadel, calling out for the columns to advance. This they immediately did; and as the enemy,

certainly not aware of the mine, or, at least, of
its immediate explosion, had suffered severely, the
column met with no material resistance until they
filed off to the right and left of the bastion.　Then
the light companies, under Major Everard, were
obstinately opposed upon the ramparts, insomuch
that there was a momentary check.　But nothing
could long resist the bravery of that fine corps
and their leader, and, surmounting every obstacle,
they pushed on, clearing bastion after bastion.

My corps having been drawn up close to the
fort, I quietly stole up to the walls, and witnessed
the bravery displayed by the right escalading
column under Colonel Delamaine; which equalled
my full idea of British valour.　This breach (at
the Juggernaut gate) was most gallantly defended; yet, in spite of the most obstinate resistance, our men, overthrowing every obstacle,
mounted the breach, and planted on it the colours
of the 58th N. I.　At this very time the right
column of the 14th, had just reached the Juggernaut gate; and a most furious struggle took place,
as was testified by the dead bodies literally lying
in heaps, which we saw here next day.　This
column then pushed on, clearing the ramparts,
and never halting until they met with their brave

comrades of H. M.'s 59th, at the Koombhere gate, where both corps mutually cheered each other.

A party of this (right) column had penetrated into the heart of the town; and in driving the enemy into the citadel, they pursued them so closely that the enemy were obliged to shut the gates against a large body of their own men: thus a furious rencontre ensued at the bridge. It was here that gallant officer Major George Hunter distinguished himself so conspicuously in a single combat with one of the Bhurtpore chieftains; and had he not been well supported by his men, his bravery would have cost him his life; for in guarding a blow made at him, his sword broke; and in endeavouring to defend himself with the scabbard, he received a severe wound in the left arm; when at the critical moment, some of his sepoys ran up and bayoneted his antagonist in the act of striking another blow. The rest of them, assisted by the 14th, put all the rest to the bayonet, as the citadel bridge showed well next morning, being absolutely covered with dead bodies.

Being obliged to remain near my corps, I had had no opportunity of seeing the success of the left or main column, and the intermediate or escalading one. But from all I heard, their gallantry was not less conspicuous than that of the two columns whose valour I witnessed; for, on going back to my corps, I saw the enemy actually throwing themselves from the high walls into the ditch, to escape from their brave antagonists. A dismounted squadron of my corps under orders of Captain Martindell, my second in command, had been directed with some guns, just before the mine was sprung, to advance up to the fort, and thus divert the enemy's attention. They drew a smart fire from the citadel; but not having orders to advance, they waited until one storming party got in, and opened one of the gates, when they joined the assailants, and shared in the honours of the storm. Immediately after the mine was sprung, a perfect roar of cannon and musketry commenced, and was most vigorously maintained on both sides for three hours; by which time the town was completely in our possession. But the citadel held out till four P.M., when it surrendered.

Thus fell Bhurtpore, the pride and glory of Hindostan. That fortress, which had hitherto been considered impregnable, and had even bid defiance to British power, now lay prostrate at the foot of

British valour. Nothing, indeed, could exceed the cool and steady courage of the troops, who seemed invincible; but having been an eye-witness of the bloody and disastrous scenes which passed before the fortress in the days of Lord Lake, I could not help contrasting the two sieges, and observing the shameful decline which had since then taken place in this once unrivalled state. In those days, as it is well known, we had to fight our ground inch by inch as we approached the place; while now, so different was the spirit or skill of the defenders, that we took up our ground on the very glacis, close to the ditch, without the smallest opposition on the part of the enemy; and the breach once practicable, what force of theirs could have successfully opposed Lord Combermere's fine army? a force powerful enough to conquer the whole of Hindostan. Even the brave men who fought Lord Lake would have vainly tried to oppose it, when once on equal terms. But Lord Lake and his most gallant army had obstacles to encounter which did not now exist. His acts, and those of heroes whom he led, require no mention here: they stand immortal and unrivalled, and ever must do so. And had it not been for most unto-

ward circumstances, his success here had been
certain. In the present siege, though nothing
could surpass the gallantry of the *veterans* of
Bhurtpore, the younger soldiery and their leaders
gave them no assistance. These veterans did
all that men could do; they only gave up the
place with their lives, as their dead bodies covering
the ramparts unanswerably proved; they faced
the European soldiers with " the cold steel," as
their antagonists themselves declared; but this was
all too late: the breach once won—the ramparts
gained—who could withstand the British troops?
It is on others, and especially on their cowardly
leader, that the blame and the shame rests. Doorjun Lal, instead of heading his veterans, as Run-
dheer and Runjeet did of old, and striving to
oppose the storming columns, remained inactive;
committing the fate of his city and his fortunes to
the care of others; and when he did move out
and expose himself, the time was past; the
breach was carried; the British troops had gained
their footing, and the town was their own. His
young chieftains, followers, and flatterers all left
him in the hour of need, flying as best] they
could; and Doorjun Lal himself soon followed
their example.

Taking his two Ranees and children, and mounting them behind some of his most faithful body-guard, he attempted to dash through our lines; but our cavalry were on the alert, and Lord Combermere's arrangements in disposing them round the fortress were too well made to admit of his escape. In a fit of despair, as a last resource, he made one gallant charge, and tried to cut his way through a squadron of the 8th Light Cavalry, under Lieut. Barber. But this proved too hard for him; and to save his life, he surrendered with his followers, and was carried into camp as a prisoner.

Since the death of Rhundeer and Runject Sing, the chiefs who had fought Lord Lake, the rulers of Bhurtpore had been given up to luxury and dissipation in the greatest excess. They were addicted to the lowest vices; and the young soldiery pursued the example of their superiors. Of this description was Doorjun Lal the usurper of the government, who, instead of encouraging a spirit of military enterprise amongst his young followers, was their leader in every species of vice. Inexperienced himself in the art of war, he kept them equally ignorant of military matters, and the state fell entirely into the hands of a parcel of writers of the *Khyte* caste, the shrewdest and most dishonest knaves in Hindostan.

No one was better aware of the state of affairs at Bhurtpore; of the usurpation of its throne, and the imprisonment of its lawful Rajah, Bulwunt Sing, by his uncle Doorjun Lal, than Sir David Ochterlony; a man who was an honour to his profession and to the Government he served. He knew of every intrigue amongst its chieftains; and, from what I know of his information, I have no hesitation in saying that he would have got possession of Bhurtpore without a shot being fired, had he been permitted to pursue his own plan of operations; but, for reasons of which I am ignorant, the army assembled under his command was broken up, and another course pursued.

The strength and reputed riches of Bhurtpore were celebrated, and almost proverbial, in Hindostan. Its imagined impregnability had been confirmed in the opinion of the natives by the repeated failures of the gallant army under Lord Lake. "Ah! you may bully us, but go and take Bhurtpore," was a common expression among the petty chiefs and refractory rajahs we had frequently to reduce. Of its riches the most wonderful tales are told; and, in fact, from the universal feeling of its security, it had become the depository of great treasures, sent there from a very remote period in times of trouble and disturbance. The writer of this has heard it asserted by several persons, but particularly by a native of high rank and respectability, who was intimately acquainted, and, indeed, connected, with all the affairs of Bhurtpore, that, while besieged by Lord Lake, the Rajah being hard pressed for money to pay his troops, in this dilemma sent for the Chowdry, or head man of the Chumars (or skinners, a low and unclean caste), and told him of his wants. The man inquired into the nature of his difficulties, and being satisfied of their reality, he took his people to a certain spot, where, on digging, they found a store of three lakhs of gold mohurs (equal to 600,000*l*. sterling), and a number of brass guns.

The Rajah was very thankful; but expressing a desire to know whether, if wanted, this assistance could be repeated, the Chowdy inquired what his daily wants might be? The Rajah said about a lakh of rupees a day, on which the Chumars replied, "Fight on, then, Maha Rajah, with good heart, for two years, if it be needed, and we will find you the means."

It may not be very generally known, that in India, where of old, in the often changing times, the rich natives used to bury their treasure in specie—a practice which may, in some degree, account for the remarkable absorption in that country of the bullion which has always been flowing into it — and in order to preserve the record of such deposits in case of accidents to themselves, the secret of their places of conceal-ment was confided to the low and degraded caste of the Chumars—the skinners of dead animals—the scavengers, as it were, of the community. The reason for making this choice at first was no doubt the very circumstance of their degradation, which forbade the hope of rising, and, therefore, took away the temptation for appropriating the wealth thus confided to their charge. The event has proved the correctness of the reasoning; and the feeling of confidence reposed has given birth to an *esprit-de-corps*, even amongst this wretched class, which has prevented the trust from having ever been violated. The only occasions on which they were permitted to discover and make use of this ancient treasure, were in cases of great state difficulties, as in that above related; and there is no doubt that there is a vast amount of buried treasure, not only at Bhurtpore, but over all India.

A circumstance of this sort was related to the writer by the same person who told him of what had passed at Bhurtpore. Not very long ago—that is, in his knowledge as a grown man—on pulling down a wall of the old palace at Biana, a town belonging to the state of Bhurtpore, there was found a slab of marble, under which were discovered a number of gold pieces, bearing the impression of the emperor Allah-u-deen Ghoree. The matter was hushed up at the moment; but for seven days afterwards 100 camels daily were sent from Biana to Bhurtpore, and 50 on the eighth day; in all 750 camel loads of some heavy substance. What it was—whether gold, silver, or lead—was not known; but my informant himself was witness to the number of loads, and the natives believed them to be of gold. This, probably, may not have been the case; but the fact was understood to be incontestible.

It may be thought strange that when these Chumars are so well known to be the depositors of so much hidden treasure, the chiefs or kings of the country should not by some means force the

secret from them.   But such is their fortitude
and peculiar point of honour, that when this has
been attempted they have always suffered torture
and death in preference to betraying their ances-
tral trust, which, in fact, has something of a
religious sacredness attached to it; and on one
occasion no less than fourteen Chumars were thus
put to death.   It is said that Diaram, the Rajah
of Hattrass, succeeded by a stratagem in obtaining
some money from the Chumars of that fortress,
and in cheating them out of their customary fee.
They had agreed to furnish him with a small sum,
on his paying them their due and granting them
his protection; and this he in the first instance
honestly performed.   But on the next application
a larger store was pointed out to him, when he
refused to part with a shilling of it to them.   We
believe they foretold his ruin from this piece of
perfidy.

After the fall of Bhurtpore, negociations were
opened by Sir Charles Metcalfe with the Alwar
Rajah, who had slighted and disobeyed the Resident's authority, and no satisfactory reply having
been elicited, Lord Combermere marched with
Sir Charles to the Alwar frontier.   The demonstration was enough.   The example of Bhurtpore

sufficed—the Rajah came into camp, and having first paid part of the expenses of the expedition, agreed and signed every condition required of him, and then was permitted to depart in peace. The army then broke up, and Lord Combermere reviewed the several divisions. Among the rest, my two corps had the honour of an inspection, and his Excellency, on taking leave of them, was pleased to address them in a most handsome speech, intimating his high satisfaction with their services, which he would not, he said, fail to bring to the notice of the Honourable Court of Directors. We then gave his lordship a grand entertainment,* in token of our high respect, and the sense we entertained of his uniform kindness, and finally bade him adieu.

While on our march back from Bhurtpore, I learned that Lord Combermere had received from the Court of Directors an order to disband three of the new local corps of cavalry, of which my second corps was to be one. Alarmed at this

* This entertainment was given at his jaghire of Belospore, to which place Lord Combermere came to visit him, with all his staff and camp followers. It was an ample feast, and served in true Hindostanee fashion. We have heard, on good authority, that Skinner, with his own hands, carried a dinner to the lowest drummer in the camp!

news, I hastened back by dawk to see his lordship, and to represent the extreme hardship which
such a measure would inflict upon my poor men.
A year had scarcely elapsed since the corps was
embodied, and the poor fellows were of course
still deeply in debt from the purchase of their
horses, arms, and uniforms, so that the present
orders, if carried into effect, must cause their utter
ruin.   Happily, I found his Excellency too fully
sensible of the worth of the corps and of the value
of their services, and too much alive to the obvious
injustice of the measure, to have much difficulty
in securing his influence in their favour.   He made
a strong remonstrance against the orders of the
Court, and procured a very favourable modifica-
tion of them.   Recruiting was put a stop to in the
corps ordered to be disbanded, and they were
permitted to die off, instead of being abruptly discharged.   But my first corps was reduced to the
peace establishment—that is, to 800 instead of
1,000 men; the native officers of the reduced
troops being, however, retained as supernumer-
aries, until absorbed by the effect of casualties into
the strength of the corps.

CHAPTER XVI.

*Colonel Skinner made Companion of the Bath, and Lieut.-
Colonel in H. M.'s service — Congratulation and letter
thereon—His feelings on the occasion—Repairs to Calcutta—Farewell to Lord Combermere—Goes on board the
Pallas frigate—His delight at seeing her exercise—Introduced to Lord and Lady William Bentinck—Returns to
Hansee—Feat of some of his Sowars—Death of Shadull
Khan—Joins the Governor-General as part of his escort
to Rooper—Preparations for a conference with Runjeet
Sing—The Maha Rajah's camp and arrangements—The
meeting—Ceremonies—Presents—Return of visit—Reception by Runjeet—Review of British troops—Of Runjeet's
troops—Their appearance and condition—Review of British horse artillery—Entertainment given to the Governor-
General—Return by his Excellency to Runjeet—Army
breaks up—Tour of Governor-General into Rajepootanah
—Reception of different Rajahs, and of Ameer Khan—
Ceremonies and presents—Large body of Rajepoots assembled—Degraded state of the present Rajepoots—Lord
Clare presents Colonel Skinner with a sword—Lord William Bentinck presents him with a superb vase—Inscription thereon—The Colonel's feelings thereupon—Lord
William Bentinck's public letter to Colonel Skinner on his*

IN this year I had the gratification to learn that
his Majesty, at the recommendation of the British
Indian Government, had been graciously pleased
to confer upon me the most Honourable Military
order of the Bath.* I understand objections
were started as to my eligibility to the same, as
having no other than the Company's local or
temporary rank in this country: upon which his
Majesty was further pleased to declare, that " this
officer has so often been brought to our notice,
that his services must no longer be neglected;
therefore, let the gift of rank be bestowed by the
Crown."

To his Excellency Lord Combermere, I feel
especially indebted for this mark of his Majesty's
approbation, as his lordship, after the siege of
Bhurtpore, promised to bring my services and
that of the corps to the particular notice of the
Honourable Court of Directors; and it was at
his lordship's recommendation that his Majesty

* That is, Commander of the Bath.

was pleased to confer it upon me. But it would be ungrateful in me to omit the expression of my thanks to Mr. C. W. Wynne, of the Board of Control, for the generous interest he took in my favour, and the more especially as I was to him a perfect stranger.

When the efforts of my first most worthy and lamented patron, Lord Lake, and, subsequently, those of the Marquess of Hastings, failed of obtaining for me rank, I had little expectations of ever receiving any further acknowledgment of my past services, and far less so brilliant a reward as has now been so graciously conferred upon me; and my feelings on first receiving the intelligence may be more easily imagined than described. I can only say, that my utmost endeavours shall now be directed to render my future services equally deserving the approbation of my sovereign and my honourable employers as hitherto; and though old age is creeping fast upon me, I trust that the Almighty may yet spare me to lead my " yellow boys " again into action; for I could not desire a more honourable end to my career than to close it at their head as I commenced it. Such, too, is, I know, the ambition of my brave veterans, to whose valour and fidelity alone I owe all the honours that have come upon my age, and who would seek no better than to fall in the faithful discharge of their duty.

The following letters explain at once the immediate agency by which this act of real justice was brought about, and the kindness and perseverance of the friends who exerted themselves to obtain it. The first is from his old and warm friend, Sir John Malcolm, to a relative of Colonel Skinner.

" My Dear Wood,—The accompanying is a copy of my last book, for my excellent friend, James Skinner; pray forward it. I have written him by the packet. I owe you many thanks for your kind letter about him and my favourite ' yellow-boys.'

" I have great pleasure in assuring you that he is appreciated here. I have done all I could ; and was glad to find (in a conversation I had yesterday with Mr. Charles Wynne) that it was intended to make him a Companion of the Bath. There has been some difficulty* about his not having a king's commission. Mr. Wynne seemed disposed to recommend

* When Mr. Wynne observed that the only obstacle to his being made a C.B. was his not having a king's commission, Sir John said, " Then why does he *not* hold a commission ? Has any officer deserved it more ? Out of the

that being given him also, as a double honour; and you may be sure I encouraged the idea. It may or may not take place; but it shews the disposition, and something, I trust, will be done. I shall be a ' flapper.'—Yours, &c.

(Signed)   " J. MALCOLM."

Both of these objects were attained, as we have seen; and Skinner received the rank of Lieut.-Colonel in H.M.'s service and the Companionship of the Bath, as intimated to him by Lord Combermere. But from some irregularity which seems never to have been perfectly explained, his rank was not put in orders in India. Of this Skinner complained both to Lord Combermere and to Lord Dalhousie. The following letter is in reply to one which had been addressed to the last nobleman:—

Calcutta, 15th June 1830.

"MY DEAR COLONEL,—Although I have been now very long a sufferer under this hot climate, and lately

numerous individuals in Spain and Portugal to whom brevet commissions have been granted, mention *one* who has done the same service to the state?" This was unanswerable, and Skinner was made Lieut.-Col. and C.B. It was, in fact, Sir John Malcolm and Lord Combermere who carried the matter through against not very creditable opposition.

so ill, as to be totally unable to write, or even to hold
my pen, I did not neglect your letter; and I think the
General Orders will have already reached you to put
all future misunderstandings on the subject out of the
question. Why Lord Combermere did not at first put
your commission in orders, I cannot clearly understand; but that has been the cause of all your mortification; my hopes yet persuade me that I may
accomplish a journey to Simla.—Believe me, yours
very truly,

(Signed)   "DALHOUSIE."

The next letter from Lord Combermere must
have been written before the above; but it has
no date.

" MY DEAR SECUNDER,—I am happy to inform you
that your rank is confirmed; that is, you are to take
rank as Lieutenant - Colonel with all colonels in
H.M.'s and the Honourable Company's Service,
according to the dates of your respective commissions.
I wrote home, if you recollect, from Simla, recom-
mending the above. When you come here, I will
show you an extract of a letter from the Court of
Directors* conveying the above, which will gratify

---

* There is no doubt that the opposition and the delay lay
mainly in Calcutta, for which see the minute which follows

you as much as it has done me, Macan, &c. It is
the best letter of the Honourable Court's that I have
ever read, and does them infinite honour; inasmuch as
their expressions of admiration and gratitude for the
faithful and gallant and important services of a
meritorious old soldier, are there warmly recorded.—
Your very sincere friend,

(Signed) " COMBERMERE."

The letter or rather minute of the Court of
Directors alluded to above, is as follows:—

" The remark made in the second paragraph of your
letter under reply, that 'your Government was not a
party to the recommendation in favour of Lieut.-Col.
Skinner to the Crown, which obtained for that officer
the rank of Lieutenant-colonel in the East Indies,' has
occasioned us some surprise; for, in your military
letter of the 20th of July 1816, you expressly recommend that the stationary as well as the then merely

in the text, and that it was Lord Combermere's resolute sense
of justice and friendship that overcame it. When he went
to Calcutta, and found that the promotion had been granted,
but not published, he immediately issued the order, roundly
reminding the authorities that the Company's officers had
no rank save what was granted by the Crown, and if they
disputed this right of the Crown, they would be commanded
by any ensign in the King's service.

nominal rank of Lieut.-Colonels Skinner and Gardiner, and the stationary rank of Major to the then nominal Major Skinner, should be granted, to which we acceded.

"It is true that in your letter of the 26th June 1819, you withdrew your recommendation in Colonel Skinner's behalf, as you considered it to be no longer necessary for the public interest; but the only objection you then made to the principle on which your former recommendation had been founded was, ' that the measure would not prove acceptable to the officers of the army.'

" In the same letter, you informed us that the rank of brevet-major had been assigned from the Horse-Guards to Major Gardiner, without any notification to us of such objections to that grant as you now think apply to a similar concession to Lieut.-Colonel Skinner; yet we think it must have occurred to you, that, if Major Gardiner acted upon the rank then conferred upon him, he must in all general duties have commanded all officers of H.M.'s and our service of inferior grade, but must have even superseded his immediate superior, Lieut.-Colonel Skinner, that officer's rank being then only nominal.

" We state these circumstances for the purpose of explaining why, when Lieut.-Colonel Skinner was again recommended to his Majesty for the brevet-rank which has since been conferred upon him, no objection to that measure was offered on our part. The object of granting the commission of lieutenant-colonel in the East Indies to Lieut.-Colonel Skinner, was, as you rightly apprehend, with a view to qualify that officer for the distinguished honour conferred on him by his Majesty, as a Companion of the Bath.

" We regret that the granting of that commission to Lieut.-Colonel Skinner should, even for a moment, have produced unpleasant feelings in the minds of our military officers.

" Lieut.-Colonel Skinner, holding from his Majesty the local rank of Lieut.-Colonel in India, must necessarily entitle him to all advantages arising from the possession of his commission; and, consequently, to take rank according to the date of it, with the officers of the king's and of our service.

" We feel ourselves bound to direct, in justice to that distinguished officer, that you should take no measure with reference to him or the corps he commands, which you would not have taken had he not received from his Majesty the local rank of Lieutenant-colonel in India.

" Lieut.-Colonel Skinner must not suffer in his professional prospects in consequence of his having

deserved and received a peculiar mark of his Majesty's
approbation; and we are assured that there is so much
of high and honourable feeling amongst our military
officers, as to lead them not to question the advancement of a good soldier, who has won his honours in
the field.

"We cannot conclude these remarks without
expressing our surprise, that in cases such as that
before us, involving in your opinion a great military
embarrassment, you had not thought proper to consult
your Commander-in-chief upon the subject, on which
his personal sentiments would have been particularly
acceptable to us."

Extract General Military Letter,
27th March 1829.

In the year 1828, Lord Combermere again
visited the upper provinces, and coming to Hansee, in November, took occasion, after an inspection of my corps, to announce to them the
honour that had been conferred on me, in the
following speech:—

"I have," said he, "a most pleasing duty to
perform, and I take this, I fear, my only opportunity of doing so in presence of your distinguished
corps. I have to inform you, Colonel Skinner,
that our beloved and revered Sovereign has been

graciously pleased to confer on you the companionship of the most honourable Military Order of the Bath, for the long, faithful, and meritorious services rendered by you to the Honourable the East India Company.

" I am confident that all the officers, non-commissioned officers, and soldiers in the 1st Local Horse will be gratified, and will feel a just pride in knowing that their gallant and faithful conduct upon all occasions is not unknown to, and has been thus rewarded by his Majesty in the person of their respected and adored commander. It would have added much to my own gratification had I been enabled, by the arrival from England of the decoration, to invest you with the insignia of the Companionship of the Bath, at the head of your corps." And when all this was explained to the corps the men congratulated me with three cheers, and appeared quite proud of the honour.

In 1829 I repaired to Calcutta, to take leave of Lord Combermere on his departure from the country, and repeat my grateful acknowledgements for his unvarying kind attention to myself and my corps. By him I had the honour of being introduced to Lord and Lady William Bentinck, from whom I received, during my stay at the presidency, the most flattering attention.

I accompanied Lord Combermere on board the *Pallas* frigate to the Sand Heads, and never having before been on board a ship of war, was infinitely struck with what I saw. During my stay of four days on board I was most kindly treated by Captain Fitzclarence, who commanded the vessel, as well as by all his officers. Captain Fitzclarence was obliging enough to treat me with the spectacle of a sham-fight, and showed what a British frigate could do in action. To me, who had never witnessed anything of the sort before, all seemed like magic, and I was quite astonished to see the dexterity with which the vessel was manœuvred —after a continued roar of cannon and musketry you might the next moment have heard a pin drop, on the order to cease firing being given; and everything was kept in such order, that too much praise cannot be bestowed on Captain Fitzclarence, for the discipline preserved on board his ship.

At length I was forced to take a final leave of all my kind friends, and especially of Lord Combermere, whose unceasing goodness I never can forget. As a last act of kindness, he insisted

on presenting me with his own insignia of the
Bath, as my own had not arrived; and he did not,
he said, like to leave the country without seeing
me invested. I could no longer control my emo-
tions, but left the ship with my eyes full of tears.

About the middle of 1829, an epidemic broke
out at Hansee, by which I lost a number of my
oldest and most valuable native officers; while
at the same time orders were received from
the Court of Directors, in reply to the reference
made concerning the disbanding of the three local
corps, repeating their commands for this reduction.
I consequently lost my second corps, and it was
with great difficulty that Government, at my most
earnest request and remonstrance, sanctioned the
settlement of a reduced pension on those native
officers and men whose service was of twenty years'
standing; and as I had been obliged to draft or
promote a number of men from my first to my
new corps, I lost many of my most valuable soldiers
by this reduction.

In the year 1831, a party of thirty sowars of my
remaining corps, under command of Bajazeed Khan
Jemmadar (son of a veteran who died in the corps),
distinguished itself very honourably in discharge
of the duty entrusted to it. Being posted at

Bahul, a frontier point, information was sent to tell them that a strong body of Kozaks, or plunderers, had driven off a herd of camels from our territory into that of the Baraitches. The detachment saddled instantly, overtook and cut up a number of the robbers, and rescued the camels. These being left in charge of one-half the party whose horses were fatigued, the other half continued in pursuit of the plunderers, and followed them up to a Baraitch village, from the people of which they expected that assistance which it was their duty to afford. Instead of this, however, the whole village turned out, joined the robbers, and surrounded the few of my sowars who first came up. One of their horses which was knocked up dropped down with his rider, and the Zemendars with a yell rushed on to destroy him; but his companions, nothing daunted, sprang forward to his assistance, and in spite of the enormous disparity of numbers—they being full 500, while of my men there was only about a dozen—they rescued the fallen trooper, and after a desperate skirmish made good their retreat with the loss of only one sowar killed, and another, with two horses wounded, that of the villagers amounted to fully fifty in killed and wounded; and so sickened were they of the taste of my men's steel, that they did not venture to pursue the party.

At this time Skinner records, in terms of deep feeling, the death of Shadool Khan, that old and most trustworthy officer, to whose care, at the . expected storm of Bhurtpore, he had entrusted his son James. We do not venture to give the passage: but it affords a touching proof of the kindly and patriarchal footing on which he ever stood with his men, and the great interest he took in the affairs of every individual among them. On this occasion, he wished to place the son of the deceased officer in the corps as a " duffadar," or commander of ten, because he knew that it would be a gratifying compliment to the whole corps—a boon, as it were, to their *esprit du corps* which would have had a powerful and excellent effect—and he regrets that, from the extreme youth of the boy, it was not deemed proper to grant his request. It is difficult for official people to break through established rules, even for the attainment of a desirable but insulated object.

In the latter end of 1831, he continues, I was directed to hold myself in readiness with a squadron, or two rissallahs of my corps, to join the grand camp about to be formed at a place called Rooper, on the banks of the Sutlej, where a meeting was to take place between the Governor-General Lord William Bentinck and Runjeet Sing, chief of Lahore. It was Lord William's wish to show the Sikh chieftain a specimen of each branch of the British Indian army; and previous to his lordship leaving Simlah the undermentioned troops were ordered to march to Rooper, the whole to be under the personal command of Brigadier-General Adams, viz., two squadrons of his Majesty's 16th Lancers, his Majesty's 31st Foot, the 14th Native Infantry, a troop of Native Horse Artillery, and two rissallahs of my corps, besides his lordship's body-guard.

We left Hansee on the 1st of October, and marched by Kurnaul to Rooper, which we reached on the 21st, and found General Adams already there, busily employed in clearing a large piece of ground for the encampment, in the front of which was a fine level parade, made to extend from the camp to the bank of the river, and occupying a space of at least two square miles. On his lordship's arrival, a daily piquet was put on duty, and a chain of sentries planted at night, just as if we had been before an enemy; and Runjeet was particularly struck with this strictness of our discipline. A field-officer was daily appointed for duty, and had to go the rounds regularly at night, and visit each piquet and sentry. This was the first time I had the honour of commanding British troops, as the General had ordered me to be placed on the roster of duty as a field-officer.

Preparations were likewise carried on upon the opposite bank of the river; and Runjeet's men had cleared a fine space and planted a garden, in the centre of which the royal tent was to be pitched. Wheat had been sown, too, in the shape of men, birds, horses, &c., in which forms it came up for the amusement of the chief, as well as to give verdure to this royal and magnificent encampment, as the place cleared out for the Maha Rajah's tent was under a barren rock, though on the bank of the river. A bridge of boats was likwise prepared by the Maha Rajah's people; and though the boats were very small, it was yet sufficiently strong to allow the royal sowarees, consisting of elephants, horses, &c. to cross to and fro; nor did a single accident occur during the whole time of the meeting.

After his lordship and suite had arrived from Simlah, and all our encampment had formed, the royal tent and the Maha Rajah's superb peish-

khanah * arrived, and was pitched in the centre
of the newly-planted wheat-garden.   The royal
tent was made of red broadcloth, and the kunnauts, or curtains, which extended on each side to
the river, leaving the front view open, were made
of yellow silk and satin, with an entrance resem-
bling the gateway of the royal palace at Dehlee,
so that elephants with howdahs might pass under
it.   Besides the royal tent, there were two or
three smaller ones of rich cloth, &c., as also a
silver bungalow or pavilion, something in the shape
of a Hindoo temple, about ten feet square.   This
was placed on a hill in a very conspicuous situation, so as it might be seen very plainly from our
encampment, and was carried about and placed as
suited the different ceremonies and occasions.

On the 25th of October, about eight A. M., his
highness marched in, and the arrival was announced by a royal salute and discharge of 101
guns from the Maha Rajah's artillery.   Their
encampment occupied a large space of ground, as
the troops were scattered in their tents all over
the country, in order perhaps to give them a
more formidable appearance.   The force accompanying Runjeet was, however, pretty much as

* The people and preparations sent in advance.

follows, viz. 16,000 horse, seven regiments of infantry, and twenty-one guns, of which, however, more hereafter. In the mean while, I shall give an account of each day's occurrences.

Immediately on the Maha Rajah's arrival, a deputation, consisting of Mr. Prinsep, General Ramsay, and two other officers, with sixty sowars from Skinner's horse, was sent over, and received by the Maha Rajah with a salute of fifteen guns. After which, his son, Khurruck Sing, paid the Governor-General a visit, and was received with a salute of seventeen guns. He took his leave at noon.

On the 26th, the Maha Rajah paid the first visit, and all our troops formed a street from the Governor-General's tents toward Runjeet's camp. He arrived at nine A.M. escorted by 1,000 horsemen, dressed in silk and velvet, and with rich armour. As he passed along, each corps saluted; the Company's colours only dropped. The Governor-General, with all his suite, received him about 100 yards from the Government tent. After going through the ceremony of talking and asking after each other's health, about 200 trays were brought forward, filled with shawls, silks, velvets, keenkhaubs, salahs, and other manufactures;

together with several double barrelled guns and
pistols, two horses, and two elephants; which
were all presented to the Maha Rajah. About
ten he took his departure, which was announced by
a royal salute of twenty-one guns from our side.
On his arrival at his own camp, his men received
him with about fifty guns. Of the horsemen of
his suite, about 200 were good, the rest very
indifferent. The French Lancers were only a
mockery as to discipline, their horses were inferior,
and they were badly armed.

On the 27th, about seven in the morning, his
lordship returned the Maha Rajah's visit. Khurruck Sing, his Highness's eldest son, met his
lordship about a mile on our side the river.
When he crossed the bridge of boats he was met
by Runjeet Sing and all his sirdars. His lordship
shook hands and went into the Maha Rajah's
howdah. They then passed along a street of
fully a mile long, formed by his infantry and
cavalry. The Durbar was surrounded with large
silk kunnauts, enclosing a space of about 2,000
yards square. In the middle of this was pitched
the royal tent, made of scarlet broadcloth, and
lined in the inside with yellow velvet, worked
with gold; the carpets were all rich and superb

shawls.   Horses unmounted were arranged in ranks in different places.

His lordship, on dismounting from his elephant, received a salute of twenty-one guns, and was seated on the left of the Maha Rajah; his son, Khurruck Sing, was on his right; about twenty sirdars, richly dressed and armed, succeeded, and their own officers according to their respective ranks.   Captain Wade sat a little before Runjeet Sing, and acted as interpreter between him and his lordship.   He was also master of the ceremonies, as long as the interview lasted.   About 300 sirdars were introduced to his lordship, good-looking men, and richly armed.   After them our officers were introduced to the Maha Rajah.

When we had all been introduced, the sirdars removed to a separate tent; and then came a band of about 100 young women, well dressed and jewelled, who, after saluting us, sat down upon our left: some had arrows in their hands, and some had bows—the commandant bore a staff of order.   They all wore yellow turbans inclining to one side, which gave them a very imposing appearance.   After singing a short while, they also retired; and then came the Maha Rajah's presents, consisting of about 100 trays of the manufactures

of the country.   A string of pearls was put round
Lord William's neck, by Runjeet himself, and two
horses and an elephant were brought forward and
accepted by his lordship.

He then got up and looked at all the magnificent tents, &c. and afterwards took leave of the
Maha Rajah, under a salute of the usual number
of guns.   Everything was well arranged, and in
the old royal fashion of India.   The Maha Rajah
was superbly dressed with jewels, and wore upon
his left arm the famous diamond called the Koh-
e-Noor.   We returned to our tents about eleven
in the forenoon.

On the 28th, at three in the afternoon, all our
troops were paraded.   Runjeet, with 200 soldiers,
arrived about four, accompanied by his lordship,
his body-guard, and staff.   A general salute was
then given, after which the Maha Rajah inspected
the whole of the troops very minutely.   Then the
manœuvres commenced, and his Highness was so
much delighted that he went about alone amongst
the troops with the greatest confidence, and asked
the general to repeat some of the manœuvres.   He
was particularly pleased with our squares.   " They
are like a wall of iron," he remarked.   About
sunset he took his leave under a royal salute,

quite delighted with all he had seen, and presented
11,000 rupees to the troops.   This evening Runjeet proved himself to be a far superior soldier to
any other native.   He seemed as if gifted with
the intelligence of an English Field - Marshal :
and, in fact, he moved about as if he was himself
in command of the troops.

On the next day, the 29th, the review of Runjeet's troops took place ; and it was as grand a
sight as I have seen since I left the Native Service.
In front of the parade was placed the silver bungalow, which I have before described ; on the top
of which sat the Maha Rajah, with the Lord and
his staff.   The rest of the officers were seated
under *Shemianehs,** pitched before the pavilion.
Before the whole of this Durbar were all the
movements performed.   There were four regiments of infantry drawn up three deep.   Each
consisted of 1,000 men, chiefly Sikhs, but having
some Mussulmen and sepoys intermixed.   This
brigade, with from fifteen to twenty gallopers,
was commanded by a Sikh general ; who, after
they had passed in review before the Durbar,
went through some of those manœuvres which

* Fly tents, or pavilions, merely to afford shade from the
sun.

were practised by our troops about a century ago. All was done in slow-time, and each manœuvre took up fully a quarter of an hour. Their firing, however, both in square and line, was very regular, and the men marched very steadily. They were all armed with muskets, and dressed like our sepoys.

Three or four of the guns, out of the number brigaded with the infantry, were attached to each battalion; and, whether in square or line, the infantry always left a space for the guns, and both fired together. The artillery were much inferior to ours; and all their movements were done at a walk. There was only a regiment of cavalry, called "the Dragoons" brigade, with the infantry; but after passing in review, they stood still on their right flank, and neither covered nor acted with the infantry. They were dressed in red jackets and steel helmets, and were armed with carbines and pistols. Monsieur Allard, under whose command they were, thinks them fully equal to our cavalry; but as far as I could see of them, I think them much inferior. The rest of the cavalry was drawn up in line on each side of the temple, and occupied, from flank to flank, a space of from three to four miles. They are by far the best of Runjeet's troops, and I think the only ones that would be useful in the field, though they are not disciplined. The whole of this body are Sikhs, good-looking men, and well mounted. They were dressed in yellow silk, and a great number wore armour. Some of these men who have distinguished themselves, receive, as Runjeet's own Bungars (Bargeers?), from 300 to 400 rupees per month.

On the morning of the 30th, the horse artillery was reviewed separately; and Runjeet was much pleased with the rapidity of their movements and firing, &c. Afterwards the howitzer practice was shown, and firing grape at the curtain from various distances. His Highness was quite astonished when he saw the shattered state of the target, and such was the interest he took in our artillery, that there was no satisfying his curiosity. Wishing to put their skill to a still severer test, he requested Lord William to have an umbrella put up as a mark near the target, a distance of about 1,000 yards, and direct the artillery officers to fire at it with round shot. The first two or three discharges being ineffective, Runjeet himself dismounted and laid the gun; but neither his Highness nor some of his best officers,

whom he desired to try their hand, were anything
more successful. Captain Campbell, of the horse
artillery, then took their place, and the first shot
he made sent the umbrella to pieces, on which a
roar of applause arose from the Sikhs.

After this, Runjeet sent for some of his best
horsemen, who went not very successfully through
the following feats—viz. firing at the bottle at
speed; taking a tent-peg out of the ground with
the spear; and cutting at a brass-pot with the
sabre. At this last exhibition, Runjeet's men
made a very poor figure, upon which the Maha
Rajah himself drew his sword and attempted immediately at speed to cut the brass-pot. Unfortunately he did not succeed; but I could not
help the less admiring his fine spirit, and bold
manner of riding and making his cuts. My men
were then called upon to show their skill in firing
at the bottle, in which they succeeded to the full
as well as the Sikhs, though Runjeet's men had
been picked for the occasion.

Yesterday evening an entertainment was given
by the Maha Rajah to Lord William and his
party, in which there was a great display of fire-
works, &c. In front of the royal tent was
pitched a Shemianeh, or canopy of velvet, richly

embroidered with gold, under which chairs were
placed for the company. The carpeting consisted
entirely of keenkhaub, silk, and other rich cloths,
superbly embroidered with silver and gold. In
the royal tent was placed a throne of gold, inlaid
with precious stones, and two bedsteads of the
same rich description, with equally magnificent
cushions. Indeed, the whole inside of the tent
was gorgeously decorated, and formed a most
perfect specimen of Indian luxury and extra-
vagance. The troop of Amazons also made their
appearance, and sat under the Shemianeh in the
centre of the company; and each set danced
alternately before the Maha Rajah, who seemed
very merry on the occasion, and was most atten-
tive to his noble guests, Lord and Lady William
Bentinck. Wine was brought in too, and very
freely distributed in golden cups to all the guests;
Runjeet taking a pretty large allowance. After he
had got somewhat elevated, a quantity of gold-dust
was brought and placed before the Maha Rajah,
who ordered the nautch girls to throw it over the
guests, in imitation of the festival of the *Hooly,**

---

* When red, purple, and yellow powders, made up in
balls, are thrown at each other by the guests at entertainments, like snowballs, until they get quite covered by the
various colours.

and he seemed much to enjoy the joke; for he also threw it at the ladies and gentlemen who sat near him, as well as at the dancing women. A number of his chieftains, too, were present, but none of them appeared to know how to conduct themselves; and instead of the manners of noblemen and gentlemen, displayed those rather of village churls.

Rich presents were brought in after the entertainment, and I believe Runjeet made offer to his lordship of one of his famous horses named *Loylee :* but of this his Excellency declined acceptance; and about ten o'clock the party broke up. On the following evening a similar entertainment was given by his lordship; and the next morning both chiefs left Rooper, and on the 1st November the camp broke up. Next day all the troops commenced their march back to their respective cantonments.

Shortly after the Rooper meeting, I was honoured with the commands of his Excellency the Governor-General to repair to his camp at Dehlee, and remain in attendance during his lordship's tour through Rajepootanah. Lord William had invited all the native chiefs of that country to meet him at Ajmere, which place his Excellency's camp reached on the 18th of January

1832. On the 23rd, Rajah Kullian Sing of Kishenghur arrived and paid his lordship a visit.
Some officers of the staff were deputed to conduct
the Rajah into camp, and a party of my sowars,
on duty with his Excellency, was drawn up before
the Durbar tent. The Rajah was received with
a salute of eleven guns, and his lordship rose from
his seat to meet him, and offered him and all his
sirdars seats. The English band of music was in
attendance, and continued playing during the
interview. After the customary ceremony of
" *uttr* " and " *paun*," the Rajah took his leave
under the same salute as on arriving.

On the 30th, Nawab Ameer Khan* arrived in
camp, with a force of two or three battalions, 2,000
or 3,000 horse, and some artillery. He was
received with the same ceremonies as the Kishenghur Rajah, except that the salute to him was of
thirteen guns, and that his lordship took an emerald
ring from off his finger and presented it to the
Nawab. A concourse of full 20,000 persons
assembled around the Durbar to witness this
meeting. Next morning his Excellency with all
his staff went to witness a review of the Nawab's
troops, and were much pleased with the various

* The celebrated partizan and freebooter.

feats of Hindostanee horsemanship which were
exhibited.   At the termination of the review,
Lord William took his own sword from his waist
and presented it to the Nawab.

The next visit, on the 3rd February, was from
Rajah Ram Sing of Kotah, who was received in
the same manner as the former chiefs; and two
days after came Jeewun Sing Rajah-Rana, of
Oudipore, with a grand Sowarree.   The deputation sent to welcome him consisted of six officers
from his lordship's staff, and the body-guard, together with a rissallah of my corps, was drawn up
in front of the Durbar tent.   The Rana was
saluted with seventeen guns, and met by his lordship, who advanced some steps and led his Highness to a throne on which the two chiefs sat
during the meeting.   The presents offered were
handsome, and included an elephant and two
horses all richly caparisoned.

The Rajah of Jeypore, Sewaee Sing, a lad of
eighteen, was received with the same ceremonies
and presents as the Rana of Oudipore.   The
Rajah of Boondee, Ram Sing, received the same
welcome as the Kishenghur man.   The Rajahs
of Jhoudpore, Jesselmere, and Bickanere sent
excuses for not appearing.

On the 8th of February, the Governor-General, accompanied by Lord Clare, Governor of Bombay, mounted on elephants and attended by their respective staffs and escorts, returned the Rana of Oudipore's visit, receiving similar presents to those which had been given. On the two following days the same visits and ceremonies were gone through with the Jeypore and other Rajahs, all of whom presented the same gifts, though the three first had received none — a compliment which obliged his lordship to invite those chiefs a second time in order to return them similar presents. These matters having been thus fitly arranged, the camp broke up, and Lord William returned to Dehlee by the way of Jeypore, Alwur, Kishenghur, and Bhurtpore, the chieftains of which places all gave grand entertainments to his lordship and his camp.

The various bodies of troops, both cavalry and infantry, assembled at Ajmere under their respective chiefs, amounted to upwards of 100,000 men, and about 200 pieces of cannon. When I was in the Mahratta service in the year '98, and met these brave Surajebunsees or " Sons of the Sun," as they call themselves, they were then in the full bloom of their pride as gallant soldiers courting enterprise, and fearless of danger. How changed were they now! Chief and follower alike reduced to poverty; degraded in feeling as in condition; the spirit of the soldier utterly departed; all remembrance of the deeds of their forefathers vanished from their minds; a single British chuprassie might have driven them in flocks. Their chiefs, instead of brave leaders, were either boys, or men sunk in vice or debauchery, guided by women or *karindahs* (agents) to whom all state affairs were willingly abandoned, provided they themselves were permitted to enjoy unrestrainedly their own vicious pleasures. To this state of affairs the Rana of Oudipore offers the only exception; and he, though like the rest reduced to utter poverty by the misrule and anarchy of past times, still maintains the appearance of a prince and a Rajepoot. On this occasion, they had an opportunity of seeing and estimating somewhat of the British people and power. The reception of the various chieftains was admirably managed; and all of them left Ajmere flattered by the attentions, and delighted by the courtesy, of the British nobleman and governor.

At Ajmere I had the honour of being introduced to Lord Clare, governor of Bombay, who had come over in order to meet the Governor-General, and his lordship was please don this occasion to present me with a very valuable sword, accompanied by the following handsome and most gratifying letter :—

"Camp, Ajmere, Jan. 27, 1832.

"MY DEAR SIR,—Your own sword has performed such good service to the British Government, that it is quite unnecessary to send you another; but I cannot resist begging your acceptance of that which I send by the bearer; being confident that whenever your services shall again be required in the field, you will use it in the service of Government with the same zeal and success against the enemies of England, which has in former and more perilous times than the present, so much distinguished your honourable career in India.   I would also beg your acceptance of it as a small proof of my personal regard and esteem; and I assure you, I set a high value on the handsome horse of your own breeding which you presented me a few days ago on the occasion of my visit to your tent.

" I unfortunately do not speak the language of this country; I must therefore beg of you to let your own horsemen know how much pleased I was this morning with their manœuvres, and the exhibition I witnessed of the skill of the whole troops.—Believe me to be, my dear sir, with great truth, your faithful and obedient servant,

(Signed)   "CLARE."

On the termination of the tour in Rajepootanah and the return of the Governor-General and his camp to Dehlee, Skinner received permission to return to his station. But the long and more familiar intercourse to which the genial atmosphere of an Indian march and camp invariably gives growth, had ripened into too powerful a sentiment of esteem and even friendship, to satisfy his lordship in permitting the old soldier to depart without some token that might embody his good will and speak to future times of their intimacy. There was, indeed, between the two men, though differing so widely as they did in colour and in rank, a powerful moral sympathy that, under circumstances so favourable, could not fail of developing itself, and resulting in the expression of that sincere and cordial feeling which they entertained for each other. And there is somewhat of this expression to be traced in the following inscription engraved upon a very handsome vase presented by his lordship to the colonel; alike honourable to him who penned and him who received it:—

"This Vase was presented by the Governor-General of British India, to Lieut.-Colonel Skinner, C.B., Commandant of the 1st Corps of Local Horse, on the completion of a tour during which he accompanied his lordship with a portion of his regiment through the states of Rajepootanah.

"In the course of this tour, the Governor-General had the gratification of witnessing the spontaneous applause accorded to superior military merit, by a people to whom the reputation of Colonel Skinner, as a brave and skilful officer, was familiar, and among whom he had displayed those efforts of early gallantry which afforded ample presage of his future celebrity.

"Desirous of conferring on so meritorious an officer some token of his personal esteem, the Governor-General has adopted this mode of testifying his sense of that sterling and unobtrusive worth which belongs in a peculiar degree to Lieut.-Colonel Skinner; and which has secured to him at once the devoted attachment of the gallant corps which he commands, the affectionate regard of an extensive society, the repeated approbation of the Government which he serves, and the distinguished notice of his sovereign. 1832."

What my feelings were, says Skinner, on receiving this most gracious and gratifying token of his lordship's esteem, it would be impossible adequately to describe; but no time can ever efface from my heart the gratitude I feel for his uniform kindness), nor the pride with which I received this testimony of his approbation; a memorial which it will be my pride to preserve and to bequeath to my latest posterity. I pray the Almighty that the feelings of pleasure which the kind attention of his Excellency and Lady William Bentinck has at all times given to me may never depart from their hearts, and that all the honours and prosperity which they so well deserve may attend them to their native home and to their latest hour.

The most interesting documents by far, however, are, in our opinion, two letters or despatches emanating from the same nobleman. The first, a public letter addressed to Colonel Skinner himself, is official in its form; the other, an extract from a minute of Lord William's to the Honourable Court of Directors, affords the most speaking proof of the *real* opinion entertained of his character and services, from a source of undoubted authority. But, apart from its value as a public testimony, there breathes through it a tone of earnest and generous feeling which seems to burst through official trammels, and speak the genuine sentiments of the heart. To such documents we need scarce entreat the courteous reader's attention; and as the latter forms an admirable summing-up of his character and talents, we have kept it for the last.

(*Service.*)

" To Lieut.-Colonel Skinner, C.B., Commanding Skinner's Horse."

9th April 1832.

" Sir,—The Governor-General being about to quit Dehlee immediately for Simla, considers it a pleasing part of his duty to intimate to you the gratification which your presence in his camp has afforded him during his recent tour through Rajepootanah.

" While your extensive experience and accurate knowledge of the different native courts rendered your advice particularly useful on several occasions, the Governor-General could not but feel the valuable accession to his camp afforded by the presence of a soldier, the celebrity of whose exploits had extended far indeed beyond the states visited by his lordship, but whose achievements were among them the theme of special admiration. Nor must his lordship omit this occasion of paying his tribute of applause to that portion of the fine corps under your command which

accompanied you. Their general decorum of conduct
and soldierlike bearing evinced that they are worthy
of their commander, whose brilliant and well-earned
reputation they seemed desirous to sustain. His lordship desires me therefore to request that you will sig-
nify to the men who escorted him during his recent
tour, the great satisfaction their conduct afforded him,
and that you will, on your part, accept his best thanks
and his warmest wishes for your future prosperity.—I
have the honour to be, &c. &c.,

(Signed)   "WILLIAM MACNAUGHTEN."
"Sec. to the Governor-General."

The following is the extract above alluded to,
from a minute of Lord William Bentinck's to the
Honourable Court of Directors :—

"Political Department, Simla, 17th May 1832.

"In the course of a long and varied service, in
which it has been my good fortune to make the
acquaintance of many of the most distinguished
officers belonging to the armies of Europe, as well
as those serving under the British banners, I do not
recollect to have met with any one engaging more
general esteem than Lieutenant-Colonel Skinner.
The records of the supreme Government bear ample
testimony to his useful and gallant conduct, so often

the subject of commendation by that distinguished commander, Lord Lake; and upon every subsequent occasion of military operations, receiving the same meed of applause from all succeeding Commanders-in-chief. He enjoyed in an equal degree their private friendship and their public respect.

"Having requested Lieut.-Colonel Skinner to afford me, in my recent tour, the benefit of his experience in the manners, feelings and habits of the people of Raje-pootanah, with a view to rendering my meeting with the Rajahs assembled at Ajmere as conducive as possible to their satisfaction and to the interests of the British Government, I then had an opportunity of witnessing the high opinion entertained of him by those who had been his companions as well as his opponents in arms when he was in the Mahratta service. Each chief was accompanied by some of the old sirdars; Meer Khan, in particular, the most distinguished partisan in the last wars, had upon frequent occasions come in contact with our brave 'Secunder Sahib' (as he is known by all), and it was pleasing to hear them narrating their former military exploits. There was this marked distinction between the two; that Meer Khan took to himself the merit of every success, while Lieut.-Colonel Skinner gave it always to the brave men whom he commanded.

"I cannot refrain from relating an anecdote told me by an old sirdar in the Jeypore service. He had a command at the battle of Buxar in 1764, and he must have been 100 years of age: but he still retained the erectness of youth, a fine martial appearance, and his faculties unimpaired. He described to me, with a manner and expression glowing with gratitude, how, in the battle of Jeypore, Colonel Skinner, then a youth leading a charge of cavalry, captured a field battery under his command; and by his humane and decided interference saved his life.

"It has not been without considerable mortification that I have seen the large jaghires that have been given to many native sirdars upon their leaving the Mahratta service, whose merits and services can bear no comparison with those of Colonel Skinner; but I only now revert to those bygone events to support me in a request I have to make to the Honourable Court, that they will allow a son of Lieut.-Colonel Skinner's to be made an exception to a recent rule confining the choice to their own officers, and to be placed in the Nizam's contingent, or one of the corps of irregular horse. His name is Hercules Skinner. He is lately returned from England, where, for the last seven or eight years, he has been receiving the education of an English gentleman. He passed five months in my camp, and from all I could learn, his conduct and character are unexceptionable.

(Signed)   " W. C. BENTINCK.
" (True copy.)
(Signed)   "W. MACNAUGHTEN."

The above request was supported by a strong letter from the members of council, Sir Charles Metcalfe and Mr. Blunt. We need scarcely add, that so impressive and touching an appeal could not and did not fail of success. The object was attained, and Hercules Skinner is now a captain, highly respected, in the contingent force of his Highness the Nizam.

Our task is almost done. Hindostan was quiet, " soldiering was over." The fire had burned out for lack of fuel, and the ardent spirits that so long had revelled in high military excitement were forced to settle down into the calm routine of peaceful life. The duty of the gallant, dashing "yellow boys," who had so long flown at high game, was now reduced to little more than keeping the peace, and now and then chastising a troublesome robber or refractory Zemeendar.

Their veteran commander, now little called upon
for active service, divided his time between his
well-beloved corps at Hansee and the super-
intendence of his jaghire, now greatly improved
by his good management; or in other affairs,
amongst which were his large and systematic
charities. "Nothing," says a dear friend of his,
in a letter to the writer, "nothing was to me
more beautiful than his great humility, to see him
with the poor sitting on the floor, and conversing
with them on their several cases. I had the
happiness to march all over the Doab with him
for near three months. We visited almost every
village, and the Zemeendars used to talk freely
over their concerns and of our rule; and all
classes, high and low, used to come to our tents, and
we went to their little forts and dwellings. At
the termination of our tour all the Zemeendars
came and paid the Colonel a visit for three days
at his jaghire of Belaspore, and were feasted in
turn. I was very ill at the time, but neverthe-
less enjoyed the trip much, and I think they were
the happiest days of my life. Your poor brother
William was often of our party, and with him we
spent many happy hours. You know Lord Combermere paid him a visit at Belaspore with his

camp followers. On that occasion, Secunder carried a dinner with his own hands to the lowest drummer in camp.

"Perhaps you may remember the singular end of the favourite charger that carried Skinner through Lord Lake's wars, and which, in a rencontre with the Sikhs, saved his life by leaping over some of them who attempted to stop his progress, when he got speared. This horse was pensioned, and had been so for some years. One morning he broke away from his head and heel ropes, and ran up to the window of the bungalow at Hansee where Skinner was sitting, neighed loudly, and dropped down dead, as much as to say, 'My end is near, I am come to take a last farewell!'

"Of Skinner's humility, and utter contempt of all assumption, I may mention one trait. When I was living with him, he always had an old spoon placed on his breakfast-table, to remind him, as he said, of his origin and early days."

"Skinner," writes another of his friends, "was a man of sincere piety, though one might have known him long without being aware of its extent, as he avoided all show. When I was with him at Hansee during the hot winds, we used to sleep in the verandah, for the sake of coolness. Long before daylight in the morning, I used to hear him at his prayers with most earnest utterance, half aloud, and he at all times expressed a feeling of deep gratitude to the Almighty for the worldly advantages that had fallen to his share, and an entire dependence on Him for the future."

Amongst the chief objects which he desired to accomplish, and which he at length attained, was the erection of an episcopal church at Dehlee. There are two motives to which the writer has heard the origin of this design attributed. He has been heard to say, that on the morning of that night of pain and misery which he passed naked and wounded on the field near Oonearah, when relieved by the Chumar woman who gave him bread and water, in the feeling of gratitude to Providence for this unexpected succour, he vowed if he should ultimately be preserved, and ever have the means, to build a Christian church. It has also been said that Skinner, when he purchased his house at Dehlee, found in the " compound," or enclosure, a mosque in ruins, which he repaired, and this having given rise to some remark, he declared, that though he respected Maho-

metans, and would be the last to destroy or dese-
crate their places of worship, he reverenced his
own religion far more, and would prove it if God
preserved his life, and he became rich enough
to do it, by building a Christian church. He
did live to perform this votive promise, and in
time the episcopal church of St. James's was
built at an expense of at least two lakhs of rupees,
or about 20,000*l.* *

Skinner, as has already been said, was a truly
good and pious man, and few were more deeply
imbued with real Christian feeling and charity.
But, thrown as he was at a very early age into
a career of incessant activity, and chiefly amongst
people of other creeds, it can scarcely be imagined
that his notions of religion were as strictly ortho-
dox and well understood as if he had remained
entirely in Christian society until a more mature
age. But the good soil was there, nor was the
good seed wanting. He had his Bible, and he
read it in the meek and earnest simplicity which
was so much his characteristic. Even the society
of the more respectable natives around him served

* Bishop Heber says 20,000 rupees, but this is an error :
the first estimate was more than 90,000 rupees, and it more
than doubled that.

to nourish his innate piety. For seeing them
zealous in their own religion, mistaken as it was,
he felt that he should not be less so in the superior
faith in which he had been born and bred.

Among these natives, as among Christians of
old, it was customary to devote large sums to
charitable and holy purposes; no doubt, in the
hope that their souls would be benefited by the
sacrifice. Skinner was no whit behind them or
any one in deeds of charity; and it was, doubtless,
in something of this spirit, mingled with sincere
gratitude for blessings bestowed, that he vowed
and afterwards built this church. In the same
spirit of piety, with a sense of modest humility
and of his own unworthiness, did he desire that
when he died he should be buried, not *within* the
precincts of his church, but under the doorway-
sill, so that all persons entering might trample on
" the chief of sinners."

As years rolled on, and Skinner's intercourse
with European society increased, and quieter
times gave more leisure for thought and reflection, the religious bent of his mind had more
play to operate freely. He read and conversed
more with those qualified to instruct him; and
that he had done so with effect and made progress

in the doctrines of the English church is certain, since he was confirmed by the Bishop in 1836, at which time also his church was consecrated; and ever after, till his death, he was most regular in his devotions, and constantly studied the Bible.

The active life which Colonel Skinner had always led, contributed, with a good natural constitution, to keep him in habitual good health; and though a diminution of the necessity for personal exertion had encouraged a disposition to fulness, with the exception of one apoplectic seizure, which did not recur in any serious degree, and an occasional visit of the gout, he had scarcely ever been annoyed with any illness; and so free from all such symptoms had he been for years, that when on the 30th of November 1841, he complained of a slight shivering fit, and though this was followed by daily small attacks of fever and ague for the next four days, no alarm was taken on his account, either by the medical men or those around him.

On the 4th of December, however, he became more uneasy, nor did he receive any relief from the medicines exhibited. Towards the afternoon he became sensible of pain in the region of the stomach, and expressed his fears that " the gout

had got into his chest." He repeatedly now exclaimed, he " did not know what was the matter
with him." Towards evening his pulse sank and
his skin became cold; a slight tremor came on,
and then, as appears, danger was first appre-
hended. There was, indeed, cause for alarm. In
less than an hour after, vomiting, which had at
first been vainly encouraged, came on, but with it
came a quivering spasm. His pulse ceased, and
all was over.

To speculate on the cause of death was useless.
The medical men, we learn, could throw no light
upon the subject. It was enough for the heart-
stricken family, that the father and the friend was
gone for ever. An account of his last moments,
written by his son, then an officer in his father's
corps, tells of the honours paid to the dead.

" We buried him with military honours. The
Hurreeana Light Infantry under Captain Campbell formed the advanced guard. I gave no orders
to our own corps, leaving it to them to come
either as private mourners (as they do at their
own funerals) or mounted. They preferred the
latter; and the recollection that this was the last
occasion on which I should ever see the " yellow
boys" together with their distinguished comman-

der (for the sight of his charger and helmet and accoutrements made all appear exactly as if he were at the head of his corps, and not in his coffin) tried my nerves sorely. And when they lowered him into the grave I could not help thinking of the conversations we frequently had about death; and the striking opinions he always expressed and maintained on that subject. 'We are just like seed, which vegetates when cast into the earth; and we return from whence we came.' Since his confirmation by the bishop in 1836, he was very regular in his devotions, and constantly studied the Bible. I sincerely hope he is now where we all wish he may be; for if happiness is to be found in the next world, no one deserves it better than my father; for he died with an upright and easy conscience, having never injured any one, and done good to thousands. We intend removing his remains and burying him in his church at Dehlee; so that it may form his monument; but I think it would be better to bury him by the side of poor William Fraser,* and build a separate monument, which would serve as a memorial both to the European and native community."

That this was the wish of Skinner himself, in

* Killed by an assassin in 1835.

spite of the singularly humble desire he had once expressed, may be gathered from a passage in a letter to the writer of this, written in the end of 1836 :—

"Dehlee, 29th Nov. 1836.

"I came here to have my church consecrated, which was done on the 21st inst. And a most handsome white marble tomb has been put over poor William. So you see, by the blessing of God, I have served *Him* and my friend too, whose memory and love remains firm in my old heart; and I only wish that when I am no more I may be laid alongside of him. . . . You wish me to give a narrative of his murder; I have neither the heart nor mind to relate the melancholy event. In him I have lost the best friend I ever had in this world; and my friendship with the world ends with him. I only wish I were lying with him."

This wish was gratified. On the 17th of January, the remains were disinterred; and were escorted by the whole of the corps and a great concourse of people to a place four côs from Dehlee called Seetaram-ka-seraee, where it was met by all the civilians and officers of the station, with a great multitude from the city.

" None of the emperors," said the natives, " were ever brought into Dehlee in such state as Secunder Sahib." And an eye-witness observed, that he never on any occasion saw such a crowd. Military honours were paid to the funeral by official command; and sixty-three minute guns were fired, denoting the years of the deceased. A funeral sermon was preached over the body, at which all the Europeans at Dehlee attended; and on the 19th of January, the veteran soldier was committed to his final earthly resting-place, beneath the altar of the church he had built, and beside the friend he had best loved.—*Placide quiescant.*

THE END.